THROUGH HER EYES

Women's Theology from Latin America

Edited by Elsa Tamez

Wipf and Stock Publishers
199 W 8th Ave, Suite 3
Eugene, OR 97401

Through Her Eyes
Women's Theology from Latin America
Edited by Tamez, Elsa

ISBN: 1-59752-499-9
Publication date 1/3/2006
Previously published by Orbis Books, 1989

Contents

Contents

Foreword

"Women . . . need a militant and combative theology . . . one which gives them theological and biblical tools to tear out by the roots the sources of their marginalization." Thus Elsa Tamez describes what the authors of this volume are about. From the boundaries they are moving to the center of theological discourse, affirming their roots in Latin American Liberation Theology while simultaneously challenging all sources that have denied or ignored women's right ". . . to be considered created in the image and likeness of God."

Doing theology from the point of view of Latin American women (especially poor women) means dealing with concrete daily experience. Not only do the "praxis of justice and the experience of God" determine the point of departure for theology. Its starting point must also be what Tamez identifies as a praxis of caring. That is, ". . . collegial relations between men and women, older and younger people and children, between all people." Community is important. But these women indicate that they are not willing to compromise their critique of imperialistic patriarchal structures for the sake of collegiality that remains hierarchical and male dominated.

The women have taken several daring steps in their move toward the center. The theological task is redefined to include an understanding of women's religious experience not only in a Christian context but also in other contexts like Candomblé, ". . . an Afro-Brazilian syncretism of traditional African and Catholic practices in which women are the religious leaders.'' Biblical interpretation involves a new process, ''. . . a faithful and renewed rereading . . .'' which allows silence (especially about women) to become a point of departure for scriptural exegesis. This new process of rereading can yield interesting discoveries about ministry—about the difference between biblically situated male and female models of prophetic ministry. Wholesome views of a woman-identified God come to the surface of Latin American women's theology, challenging the overwhelmingly androcentric character of the understanding of God present in much of the theology written by Latin American men. The trinity is reinterpreted from a female perspective giving women the right to stay in the church as they ''. . . call on God using feminine appellations . . . ,'' still affirming the Good News of Jesus Christ.

One of the most sober reminders to female theologians comes from Alida Verhoeven who observes that

> . . . we [women] are invited to increase the number of articles and books on theology—in this case, liberation theology. This effort does not really liberate us; in fact, by encouraging us to do [male] scientific work, we fall into the same trap. We see ourselves succeeding as solitary women who have achieved recognition in a man's world. By doing this we simply perpetuate the present situation.

Nevertheless, women scholars are called to a vocation. And this vocation is ''. . . to close a fraudulent era and fill this vacuum of language, image, and symbol with a conscience of creative spiritual force (collective knowledge) so that we will no longer be trapped by language, images, and symbols.'' This call to vocation is, according to Verhoeven, the start of an exodus—an exodus from all the restrictions imposed upon women, as well as women's exodus from ''. . . all the niceties we have become accustomed to.''

To do Latin American Liberation Theology from a female perspective, then, requires a kind of nakedness which allows women to realize and share the gifts of their essential being disrobed of the traditional male-defined doctrines, orthodoxies, and hierarchies that have, for centuries, robed women in garments designed by oppressive patriarchy. Using the legend of Mixcoaatl and Chimalman as an extended metaphor for reflecting theologically upon women's experience, Elsa Tamez shows the great benefit women derive by disrobing themselves of the cultural garb of patriarchy.

Without a doubt, the themes in Latin American Women's Theology resonate with those that have been at the center of Feminist theology for the past decade. Both groups explore women's spirituality, feminine aspects of the divine, women's way of ritualizing and celebrating, androcentric biases in the Bible and in the theological traditions, and women's experience across class, racial, cultural, and religious boundaries. Though the social locations of Latin American women theologians and North American feminist theologians are different, they apparently share a common concern for inclusiveness in church and society that brings social, political, and economic equality to all people, female and male.

However, for me, an Afro-American female theologian living in North America, these essays by Latin American women arouse feelings of gratitude and uneasiness. I am grateful for female voices from another part of the world that claim (as Afro-American women claim) that their liberation struggle is inextricably linked to the struggle of their poor, oppressed community (male and female) for social, political, and economic liberation. I am grateful for the attention given to the problems created for women when standards of beauty are determined by alien male values. For too long, Afro-American women's well-being has been negatively affected by standards of beauty perpetuated by such exploitative contests as "the Miss America pageant," the "Mrs. America Contest," etc. And it is indeed good news to hear Latin American women affirm what Afro-American female theologians are declaring, i.e., that the task of women's theology is to be *honestly* inclusive of poor, uneducated women of faith who struggle daily for the survival of themselves and their families.

There is, however, some uneasiness Afro-American women may experience as they encounter this group of essays by Latin American (female) Liberation Theologians. In a few of the essays brief mention is made of the need for women to deal with the issue of racial oppression in Latin America. Yet no article gives serious attention to the effects of racial oppression upon Latin American women's lives. Since the U.S. press has given attention to the issue of oppression against blacks in Brazil, North American black women are apt to have considerable interest in learning how, and to what extent, Latin American women will deal with the problem.

Nevertheless, Latin American female theologians have begun to lift their voices in behalf of the rights of women. They are adding significantly to the concert of women around the world declaring that women *will be* empowered in church and society. And this empowerment will be used in the service of poor women who are apt to be the most oppressed of the oppressed. This volume of essays attests to the truth of the observation made by the Mud Flower Collective in their book *God's Fierce Whimsy:* through it all ". . . women connect with the heartbeats of other women, are united through common rhythms, are changed by new visions, touched more deeply by one another's lives." Latin American female theologians writing and working in the liberation tradition are giving the theological world new vision. Let us hope that this world has sight enough to behold the truth vision affords.

Delores S. Williams

The Theological School
Drew University
Madison, New Jersey

Introduction

The Power of the Naked

Elsa Tamez

Let me tell you the story of the birth of Ce Acatl Topiltzin, the famous priest of the Toltecan god of life, who was later known by the name of the god he served, Quetzalcóatl.[1]

Once upon a time, according to the legends surrounding the beginnings of Toltecan culture, the Toltecs had a great chief called Mixcóatl. He was a warrior with extraordinary power; many warriors—or soldiers, as they would be called now—followed him on his conquests. After securing his position in Culhuacán and building his capital there, he began his conquest of neighboring towns. Among his conquests were the towns of Morelos, Toluca, and Teotlalpan.

Legend has it that during the conquest of Morelos, a beautiful non-Toltecan woman appeared before Mixcóatl. When she saw him, Chimalman—as the woman was called—"dropped her shield to the floor, tossed aside her bow and arrows, and stood before him, naked, without her shift." Mixcóatl, disturbed by the appearance of the woman and her unexpected nakedness, fired his arrows at her: "The first one he fired flew high, and she simply ducked her head. The shaft of the second arrow bent as it passed near her side. She easily caught in her hand the third arrow he fired at her. The fourth

---

Translated from the Spanish by Jeltje Aukema

arrow she drew out from between her legs." The great chief warrior was so surprised he did not know what to do. He withdrew to prepare and restock arrows. Meanwhile, Chimalman fled and hid herself "in the cave of a great craggy cliff."

Later, Mixcóatl went to look for Chimalman because he wanted to see her again. When he could not find her, he began mistreating the women of Cuernavaca. These women refused to tolerate such mistreatment. They said: "Let's go find her." When they found her they told her: "Mixcóatl is looking for you, and because of you, he is mistreating your sisters." When she heard this, Chimalman came out of hiding to look for Mixcóatl. When she found him, she again dropped her weapons and clothing to the floor and stood before him, naked. And, again without success, Mixcóatl tried to shoot her. Finally, seeing there was nothing else he could do, he became one with her. Their union resulted in the conception of Quetzalcóatl, the founder of one of the richest cultures of the New World, the Toltecan culture.

When reread today as an extended metaphor from a theological perspective by Latin American women, this beautiful story provides a framework for presenting women's experiences in the theological arena.

The starting point for reflection on Latin American liberation theology from a woman's perspective is a meeting held in Buenos Aires from October 30 to November 3, 1985. Twenty-seven women from nine Latin American countries met. We "bared ourselves" and set about the task of confronting and stopping the different "arrows" fired at us by our machistic society; and, we searched for ways to assist with the birth of the Christ child among us, among Latin Americans. This Son, whose Father is the God of Life, is dedicated to saving the world, liberating men and women, and building a new way for human beings to live with each other in justice, love, peace, and freedom. For all their similarities, Quetzalcóatl and Jesus Christ might be allies against the gods of war, money which produces injustice, and the gods who demand human sacrifice: against Moloch, Mammon, and Huitzilopochtli.

Mixcóatl Is Confronted with Nakedness

The story of the warrior Mixcóatl reminds us of other situations in which negative attitudes toward women have been, and still are, formed. We might mention as an example the negative attitudes found in the machistic Latin American society at the socio-economic, political, ideological, and cultural levels. The church, which is markedly masculine, does not escape criticism for its negative attitudes toward women. Theology too, from theological training, to bibliographical sources, and theological discourse, has been monopolized by men.

These situations are embodied in the character of Mixcóatl because his profession, that of a warrior, is loaded with masculine *stereotypes,* that is, popular ideas of what a man is supposed to be like. (The word *stereotype* is emphasized not because it refers to what he is and ought to be, but because he is male). These stereotypes fit Mixcóatl in that he is a powerful fighter, a dominator, a leader, and one who uses beautiful women for his own sexual satisfaction.

In the Buenos Aires meeting, we did not focus exclusively on society's negative attitudes toward women. We simply addressed these problems as they are experienced by all women; we wanted to concentrate on the progress of women's achievements, as well as women's contributions to Latin American theology. Nevertheless, we did take up the themes of violence against women (Betty Salomon and Lucia Villagrán), sexual violence, women's disadvantage in the workplace (Mabel Filippini), and others. Cora Ferro spoke briefly about the church's view of women as inferior beings as reflected in the *Eco Católico,* the official paper of the Roman Catholic Church in Costa Rica. Aracelyl de Rocchietti presented us with several issues including the protestant churches' "internal debt" toward women. María José Rosado talked with us about the important role of nuns and their difficulties as women pastors; Graciela Uribe elaborated on this theme. In the first half of her presentation, María Clara Bingemer dug at the theological roots of discrimination against women. Working toward the same end, Alida Verhoeven rejected language, images, or symbols which excluded the life experience and thought of women, youth, peoples and nations of other races and skin colors.

In these addresses, as in others, the women simply summarized what they have felt as attacks from Mixcóatl. The arrows he fires at women are commonly known as discrimination, subjection, oppression, and violence; his sharpest and strongest arrows are directed at poor women.

Mixcóatl and Theological Discourse

Let's examine the semantemes (translator's note: *semas* is a linguistic term translated as *semanteme:* element expressing idea or image) associated with the great warrior to look for a connection between them and the negative attitudes toward women found in traditional theological discourse.

Mixcóatl finally reached the point where he had imposed his power on the neighboring peoples; in much the same way, traditional theological discourse has imposed its spirit on all areas of life. This forced imposition encourages a splintered perspective, such as that of the dichotomous world view in which the spiritual is abstract, and even abstract ideas are removed from one another. Such a view separates life and the daily experience of God from theological discourse which leads to a dangerous dichotomy between the transcendent and the earthly, material and spiritual, body and soul. As María Clara Bingemer stated clearly in her presentation, this conceptualization of the world has worked against women.

Liberation theology does not remove the experience of oppression from the experience of God, or the life of faith; it has demonstrated another methodology in making its point of departure the practice of liberation within this context. Women involved in the theological arena welcome this way of doing theology; dealing with concrete experience means dealing with things of daily significance, and that means also dealing with the relationships between men and women.

When traditional theology deals with daily experience it often spiritualizes it, makes it something peripheral to theology or uses it as a concrete application of an abstract thought. Liberation theology, when done from women's perspective, not only deals concretely with daily experience, but it is the basis, the point of departure for their theological work. Thus, not only is daily experience integral to their theology, but theology is transformed by the incorporation of women's life experience, especially that of poor women. We believe that the theological point of departure is not only the praxis of justice and the experience of God, but also "the praxis of caring," which is to say that there must be collegial relations between men and women, older and younger people and children, between all peoples. The praxis of caring includes daily interpersonal experience. Theology which takes this into account opens its horizons to make room for other perspectives, such as women's perspectives.

Because it is so often presented as the only way to view the world, traditional theology is considered an imposed perspective. In our experience, when other ways of "God-talk"[2] are proposed, they are forbidden. Fortunately, within the last few years, other perspectives of God have appeared, in addition to liberation theology, voices representing Asian, African, Black, and Feminist theologies have been heard. As Latin American women we welcome these theologies; for ourselves, adding women's perspective, we claim Latin American liberation theology.

Logic, too, has been imposed upon us: not only by theology, but by Western thought in general. It is believed that the only, or rather, the best way to approach reality is through rational discourse, that is, through Western systematic logic. Other forms of expressing real life, in play, in poetry, or painting, are regarded as less serious, or even as lesser forms. It is noteworthy that in our Buenos Aires meeting, there was strong support for recognizing other approaches to reality.

Let's return now to our story. Mixcóatl is preoccupied with war, his daily contacts and constant companions are his male soldiers. His horizon is limited; his life experience is always measured by the same rhythms. His one-sided relationship to the world means that he can see things from only one perspective. As a result, he ends up thinking that because things are the way they are, of course, they should always be this way. In other words, what is, should be. Mixcóatl needs other horizons; theology and our fellow theologians, too, need new emphases and broader views to enrich them.

Liberation theology, in responding to the cries of those lost among the marginalized, by being situated in a particular place and time, and by considering history as but one of its pivotal points, reveals new horizons in its discourse. This broadened perspective is due to the inclusion of new subjects engaged in the theological task, such as women, indigenous peoples, and the blacks of Latin America. These subjects provide theological discourse with new horizons insofar as they are included no longer simply as objects of theological reflection but also as theologians doing theology.

Mixcóatl's courage should not be discounted but respected: He is brave; he is able to withstand the harshness of the mountains or the heat of the plains. He is not afraid of difficult situations; he knows how to confront other warriors. He is combative, yet he can also be compassionate with his wounded companions. Women, too, need a militant and combative theology, that is, one which gives them theological and biblical tools to tear out by the roots the sources of their marginalization. Women must vehemently reclaim and affirm their right to be considered created in the image and likeness of God. With their new theological tools they must discredit those biblical interpretations used as the Word of God to prove their inferiority; and, they must fight by tracking down new hermeneutic guidelines over which a liberating biblical reading can be worked out.

The difference between the combativeness of Mixcóatl and that of women is that whereas he wanted to conquer or make servants of others, the goal of women's discourse is the search for justice. The protagonists of the latter situation are the victims, but the great chief represents the dominators and his warfare is geared toward subjugating others. In this respect, traditional theological discourse is imposed and monolithic.

Chimalman has arrows too but, unlike Mixcóatl, she does not use them, not even in self-defense. Chimalman's weapons are armistice and analysis. They are tools for another kind of struggle, one which would show us a new way of being women and men, that is, of being sisters and brothers to each other and before God.

Chimalman Before She Became Naked

The word *chimalman* means "shielding-hand." Chimalman was named after her encounter with Mixcóatl. She was given this name because of the way she had stopped Mixcóatl's arrows. Chimalman had not had a name; she was an unknown woman, she was not a Toltecan, and thus not-Chimalman. She had to make her appearance in history, to dare to undress and confront the arrows of Mixcóatl in order to have a name, in order to be called Chimalman.

Chimalman had beauty (covered with clothes), youth, and arrows, but she did not have a name. It seems strange that she could exist and not exist at the same time. She was alone with her beauty, her youth, and her arrows; she was hidden, ignored, silenced by history, that is, by written history. It was as though she were not among the living, or that she lived invisibly. In the story we learn who Chimalman is, yet even now, we do not know who the not-Chimalman is. We can hold Chimalman up and admire her for her beauty and youth, or we can put her down and regard her as common and immoral; however, the not-Chimalman is surrounded by a haziness that keeps her from being defined.

What is it to be a woman? Since our theme was theology from woman's perspective, this was one of the central questions in our meeting in Buenos Aires. We considered woman's identity, her experience of God, and her daily religious life. Carmen Lora and Cecilia Barbechea delivered an excellent presentation on women's sexual identity. In her talk entitled, "I Sense God in Another Way," Consuelo del Prado explained her perspective on women's spirituality; Beatriz Arellano took up this same theme from the viewpoint of a Nicaraguan woman today.

Each of these contributions probed what it means to be a woman. This is something extremely difficult to define; it is encrusted with stereotypes and individual dreams of what women might be. It looks as though we are going from the sure to the unsure and from the unsure to the possible. We reject "the sure" in rejecting the definition of femininity in all the different ways it is communicated and promoted by the machistic ideology of our society. However, we need not remain in the uncertainty and haziness of being the not-Chimalman. There was general agreement among the women in trying to name and identify ourselves, not in the sense of defining exclusively feminine qualities, but in trying to discover predominant emphases or tones in women; our Final Statement reflects this agreement.

Not-Chimalman the non-Toltecan, in order to have a name and become part of history needed to meet Mixcóatl; alone, she could not have done this, nor could she have produced such a culture. Yet, in her meeting with Mixcóatl she had to be the shielding-hand, she needed to be able to withstand the attacks of the warrior, deflecting and destroying his arrows. Chimalman did not attack the warrior, she left her arrows on the floor, instead she invited him also to undress, that is, to know himself and to meet her as an equal.

It was clear in Buenos Aires that our intention was not to eliminate our male colleagues, not to put an end to present theological discourse. Our struggle, which must be passionate, is against machistic ideology, the victims of which are not only men but also the many women who are accomplices as well as victims. We also struggle against the whole oppressive system of war which kills thousands of innocent people, many of them poor. Itziar Lozano and Maruja González pointed out that, as women we must always work to join the feminist movement with popular movements. On the theological level, our hope is to re-create Latin American theology with an in depth view of "the shielding-woman," and to invite our male theological colleagues to produce theology with us, their female colleagues.

Chimalman's first move was timid. When Mixcóatl fled, she also fled, hiding herself in a cave of a great craggy cliff. Mixcóatl's confusion and his desire to meet Chimalman again were used against "lesser women." The legend tells us that in his frustration, Mixcóatl mistreated these women. Yet, this mistreatment generated such solidarity among the women of Cuernavaca that they organized themselves in order to find Chimalman. In response to the cries of these women, Chimalman returned to confront Mixcóatl, leaving the cave of a great craggy cliff forever.

Many Latin American women are already aware that taking those first steps toward placing themselves in history as protagonists means that they can never retrace their steps. In doing so, they would lose even more than they had gained. As Rosario Saavedra demonstrated, however slow the progress, the women's popular movement keeps moving forward. In the last years, many women from this continent have begun the search and conquest for a name: we want to go from being invisible to visible, from objects to subjects, from being not-Chimalman to Chimalman.

The Power of Nakedness

Chimalman, as noted above, received this name after having dared to risk an encounter with Mixcóatl. She had the audacity to bare herself before him and was able to prevent the arrows of the great chief from hurting her. What she did was wise and without precedent: it was highly symbolic.

The scene depicting the boldness of the naked woman is the point at which the story begins to move. The power she gained in this scene disarmed the man's hostile force; it surprised, confused, disturbed him, and made him retreat.

It is symbolic that in freely choosing to face Mixcóatl, the young woman was given the power to confront his arrows. This is an energetic and exquisite invitation to try, or to try again. In this respect, the audacious Chimalman and the Latin American women of today, too, are brave.

It should be noted that the beautiful Chimalman appeared on the road before Mixcóatl during a difficult time: the chief and his people were building an empire. They had just established themselves in the Culhuacán and were in the process of defeating and dominating the surrounding towns. It is during the takeover of Morelos that the woman appears to Mixcóatl. She is brave to venture out under such violent circumstances. The fact that she is not Toltecan like her would-be conqueror makes her bravery that much greater. She carried only two weapons: her arrows and her nakedness; both were important. The first was for defending herself against those who would strip or rape her (or torture her like those executioners of our repressive regimes). The second weapon—in a symbolic sense—allowed her to know herself better, and also invited the other to undress himself, that is, to unburden himself of all the privileges society had given him as their great chief. In doing so, he would have the chance to know himself as a man, and the two of them, woman and man, on an equal basis, in justice, peace, love, and pleasure, might produce a new culture with the blessing of the living god: Quetzalcóatl.

Mixcóatl's reaction to the naked woman is that of total confusion mixed, perhaps, with fascination; he feels threatened. He does not know what to do. His first response is to attack her, in other words, to act according to his training as a warrior and as one who imposes himself on others. He becomes even more confused when Chimalman is not hurt by his aggressions; her magic stops the arrows. Troubled by her nakedness and disturbed by her defense, Mixcóatl is completely disarmed; for the first time in his life, he retreats. At this point in the story, Mixcóatl is not able to undress himself. This is one of the most difficult steps to take: it implies rebirth; it also implies the death of an old way of living. This takes time and several confrontations. Thus, the first scene is repeated when Mixcóatl and Chimalman meet again.

In our meeting in Buenos Aires, some women related experiences they had had in becoming conscious of what it means to be a woman. They related pleasant discoveries about themselves, and their difficulties with work colleagues or their partners in the struggle. Nearly all of the women were already committed at some level to the popular movement or to base Christian communities. For them, nakedness meant leaving behind the trappings with which society, the church, and theology had dressed them. These were garments made according to the taste and convenience of a machistic ideology that permeates all our institutions and affects many men. The women also related accounts of their efforts to help other women in base communities or popular movements dare to bare themselves. Mercedes Pereira recounted her pastoral experiences among peasant women, and Amparo Ferrer reported on the creative work of women with peasant children in Peruvian soup kitchens.

Using her own experience, Ivone Gebara explained to us her understanding of how women do theology. Nelly Ritchie shared her approach to Christology; María Clara Bingemer presented a woman's view of the Trinity, and Beatriz Melano Cauch a woman's perspective on the Kingdom of God. These were all different ways women speak of God.

Using the example of Chimalman, we looked for models of brave women in the Bible. Tereza Cavalcanti presented us with a beautiful piece about women prophets in the Hebrew Bible, and Leonor Aída Concha spoke of Mary as a woman of the people.

The position of the women in Buenos Aires was similar to that of Chimalman, the "shielding-woman." Following her example, we left our hurtful weapons on the floor; we stripped ourselves of our imposed clothing and, in new shapes, powerful and newly born we destroyed those weapons to which we had been subject the moment we picked them up. Then, we set about to re-create theological discourse from our daily experience of discrimination, liberation, and God.

The daily liturgies were the food that strengthened and consoled us as we stood in this road on which we dared to appear. It is a difficult road made cruel by the machistic capitalist system, but at the same time it is an exciting place to be because of all the other women who have dared to appear there. Even though we are in a difficult position, we can still, as we stated in our Final Statement, celebrate in the public plaza our joy at meeting women from different professions and confessions who have the same concern for the lack of peace and justice on our continent; these are women who are committed to bringing about the Kingdom of God. On the whole, we found the meeting very stimulating; we also became aware of the lacunae in our work and of what needed to be worked on and improved upon.

It is important to point out that this meeting was not an isolated event. The positive and gratifying aspects of the meeting were the fruit of previous work: meetings planned with the help of women from base Christian communities; national meetings of women theologians; the systematization of the reflections of women in base Christian communities, of their experience of God at experiential and conceptual levels; workshops with women on the Bible and patriarchalism; meetings with peasant and religious women; and the collective work of women psychologists working in base Christian communities.

We do not know what motivated Chimalman to go out and meet Mixcóatl on the road: there must have been a reason, something that drove her to do it. Latin American reality and the rediscovery of the face of God in our own faces has, in many cases, provided the incentive for women to go out and stand in the road, to reconsider seriously their position as women, and to encourage them to "bare themselves" so that they can propose new ways of relating to men. They also need concrete stimuli such as that provided by EATWOT (Ecumenical Association of Third World Theologians) which offers us a forum for doing theology in the third world from women's perspective. We are grateful to this organization as well as to the Pastorate of Women and Children of CLAI (Latin American Council of Churches) for their able and warm reception in Buenos Aires.

Undressed to Remake History

Mixcóatl and Chimalman came together after two meetings. It was at this time that they conceived their son Ce Acatl Topiltzin. Shortly after that, before the birth of their child, Mixcóatl was assassinated by one of his captains and Chimalman was forced to flee to her homeland. The usurper took over Culhaucán and Chimalman died in childbirth. The child was born and raised in exile; he was cared for by his mother's parents. There, he assimilated his mother's culture and learned her beliefs: devotion to the god Quetzalcóatl, the god whose name he assumed and whom he, following indigenous tradition, served as high priest.

Years later, after he had been named Quetzalcóatl, he was asked to retake his father's kingdom. So it was that the young Quetzalcóatl arrived in Culhaucán and defeated the usurper. He then changed the name of the capital from Culhaucán to Tula and ushered in a new way of living. He spread the esteemed Toltecan culture far and wide and became its most renowned benefactor. He introduced into this culture the best of his mother's culture—such as the god Quetzalcóatl, the most generous god of the ancient indigenous culture. As the years went by, the story was embellished with myth. It is said that Quetzalcóatl was an extremely civilized man; he invented things which have benefited the whole world; having stolen it from the god of hell, he took corn back from the kingdom of the dead; he was the father of agriculture, of the ritual calendar, of writing, of medicine, etc.[3] During his reign there was a great abundance of everything. According to the story, "the people were very rich and they lacked nothing. No one went hungry and there was such an abundance of corn that they did not eat the skimpy ears of corn but used them for heating the baths like firewood."[4] Although the story continues with accounts of the ups and downs of his reign, we end our telling of it at this symbolic point.

When Chimalman invited Mixcóatl to undress, and he accepted, it was in order to reinvent history, that is to say, to create a history of new horizons by laying down weapons and socially conditioned clothing, and by beginning a new way of life.

Sadly enough, this is a risky activity which may result in death. Mixcóatl is assassinated by his own people, by those jealous of his power. Chimalman dies giving birth. Both die: one by the sword, the other giving life. Yet, both pave the way so that Quetzalcóatl may live and re-create history. Both symbolically and actually, life often follows and is always in tension with death. According to the legend, the fifth sun, which represents the new humanity, appeared with Quetzalcóatl. These are perfect people who possess—thanks to the god Quetzalcóatl—the perfect plant, corn. One must not forget that without Chimalman's apparition Toltecan history would have been very different. The Toltecs would still be a semibarbaric horde of Jaliscan or Zacatecan origin. Topiltzin, having been born of Chimalman and Mixcóatl, reinvented history according to his mother's people's vision of the world.

Latin American women, along with their partners, want to recreate cultural, ecclesial, and theological history, cultivating it with new hands, new seeds, new care, and new weapons in order to produce new fruit, new everyday relations, new ways of practicing our faith within the church, and new theological discourse. In summary, we hope to give rise to the sixth sun, under the protection of our Lord Jesus Christ. And, as men and women we want to be healed and to heal in each other, the so-called, "open veins" of Latin America.

Danger is always a concern. Quetzalcóatl was born and raised in exile; he suffered persecution, first through the assassination of his father, and later by the followers of the other god, the one who demanded human sacrifice. Latin American theology, too, was born and raised under the gaze of hostile powers resistant to collaboration for reproducing the new history, culture, and society we want so badly.

One of Quetzalcóatl's great virtues is his ability to spread the faith of the god Quetzalcóatl, the god of life who, according to legend, creates men and women with his own blood. The god Quetzalcóatl was incarnated into an ant in order to be able to crawl into a hill called Tonacatéptl, steal a grain of corn, and give it to human beings so that they could have food. He is a friend who teaches his creatures how to sow this corn, to work jade, and to build their homes. He voluntarily dies alongside the others so that men, women, older people, and children might move and breathe. Furthermore, he is a god who rejects human sacrifice and battles with other gods and priests who feed on human blood.

The god of the indigenous Mexican culture is the one who, as we said at the beginning, enters into coalition with the God of the Bible. The God of life, our Creator and Liberator, who through his Son Jesus Christ—incarnated in history, died and rose again to give us abundant life—leads us in the quest to recreate history and culture so that his kingdom may be visible on earth.

Jesus and Quetzalcóatl, born in exile, persecuted by their enemies, concerned about humankind, enter into an alliance to fight those foreign gods who make slaves of men and women, such as Mammon, the god of riches, the gods like Huitzilopostli, god of the Aztecs who demand human sacrifice, and Moloch, the Ammonite deity.

All of these gods still live today; they are incarnate in our system. Thus, the struggle of the gods continues, as does our own.

1

Women and the Theology of Liberation

Ana María Bidegain

I should like to present a historical view of the role of woman in Latin America. I shall focus on the notion of sexuality propagated in society by the Catholic Church, which used as mediators, in the twentieth century, women themselves, through Catholic Action—the same women who would one day help to create the theology of liberation. By way of conclusion, I shall indicate our search for new horizons—the quest for the foundation of a human and Christian relationship between men and women in church and society.

Presentation of the New World

Michel de Certeau describes one of the first images to circulate in Europe of that continent's encounter with the New World:

> Explorer Amerigo Vespucci arrives from the sea. Erect, cuirassed like a crusader, he bears the arms of his European ex-

---

This essay was originally written as a contribution to *The Future of Liberation Theology: Essays in Honor of Gustavo Gutiérrez* (Orbis Books, 1989). Translated from the Spanish by Robert R. Barr.

periences and beliefs. In the background are the ships that will bear to the West the treasures of a paradise. Before him is the Amerindian—nude, recumbent—nameless presence of difference, body stirring awake in a riot of exotic plants and animals.

After a moment of stupefaction in this antechamber of paradise, beside this colonnade of trees, suddenly the conquistador will write upon the body of this other, this female person before him. In her flesh he will carve his own history. He will make of her the storied body of his labors and fantasies. She will be called: Latin America.

This erotic, warlike image has an all but mythic value. It represents the inauguration of a new, Western purpose for writing. What is about to be scratched on this flesh is the colonization of a body by the discourse of power—the scripture of the conquistador. That conqueror will tear out this blank page, this untamed New World, and make use of it to mark down his Western desires and longings.[1]

Europeans arrived in America at the moment of the birth of the capitalist mode of production, and at the peak of their territorial, political, and military expansion. For them, woman's sexuality was mainly a motive for uneasiness. And their only thought was to curb it.

They encountered other cultures—cultures unprepared to encounter them. Two cultures, two unequal fragments of humanity, had developed in parallel, without mutual interference. They came in contact at the end of the fifteenth century, by way of the expansion of the Iberian world. Western Christendom obviously bore the responsibility for this utterly fortuitous encounter.

Amerigo Vespucci had discovered a new world, a world with a new way of life. Vespucci learned that in this land—which he would present to Europe, which he would introduce to cartography, and to which he would give his name—persons lived in harmony with nature. There was no private property. All things were possessed in common. There were no kings or political authorities of any kind. All individuals were sovereign to themselves. The publication of Vespucci's *New World* inspired Thomas More's *Utopia* (1518).

Westerners failed to grasp the tenor of the relationship proposed by their lavish hosts. When colonial man was offered native woman, he failed to grasp the implied demand for reciprocal service. After all, the conqueror had come to the new world not to serve, but to reduce it and its natives to captivity.

In this confrontation of two unequal worlds, it was Europe that gradually gained the ascendancy. Thus native woman continued to be offered as woman and mother. But the Amerindians managed to impose their cultural matrix on the conquerors. After all, the sovereign of the land, of the age-old human tradition of the soil, was the native. The Hispanic and African newcomers only transplanted the topsoil of their European and African cultural matrices.

The apparent extermination of Amerindian social and economic structures does not militate against the fact of an ethical and cultural symbiosis between conqueror and native. Both the Spaniard and the African gradually adopted Amerindian tradition, and with it acquired a knowledge of nature that was thousands of years old.[2] It was woman who taught the European new eating habits adapted to the climate. She also prescribed thousands of hygienic recipes, like the daily bath, the use of natural elements in households, and the use of native drugs in the treatment of tropical diseases. She also served the white male by bearing him offspring to swell his labor force.

Amerindian material creativity is still very much alive today, in our practices and customs, in our culinary arts, in our handicraft. Amerindian artistic creativity is present in the melancholic, sensitive, emotional folklore of the first American cultures.

We can confidently assert, then, that the mother of America is native woman. We are her mestizo children. Our Amerindian mother has bequeathed to us her cultural womb. Our task today is to rescue and value it if we hope to stand erect before the white colonial.

Woman was a captive and a slave in a number of ways. She was used as slave labor. She was used as a woman: as the master's sex object, and as the mother who reproduced a labor force for toil in the mines or on the sugar plantations and ranches.

Enslaved many times over, the Amerindian, black, mulatto, mestiza woman prolonged in America the condition of the humiliated and wronged of the system down through the ages. Hence she was fertile soil for the gospel message of life that white woman, the dominator, could only communicate mechanically in the domestic chapel.

The Amerindian male, himself humiliated and exploited, frequently escaped his situation in drink, gambling, and an insanity that could culminate in suicide. It was the Latin American woman of the people who bore, firmly and stubbornly, subtly and tactfully, the burden of humiliation and subjugation placed on her shoulders by the colonial structure.

And therefore the gospel was handed down by successive generations of women—not so much from mother to child, but from female generation to female generation, just as in the Afro-American cults today.

Among the popular masses, the mother has always been the best catechist. It was mothers who handed on to future generations their own experience of the stubbornness and silence of faith, their hope beyond hope, and their totally gratuitous charity. Of course, the values of this captive, exiled Christianity were transmitted from generation to generation by humiliated women in a nonverbal way. Word was the property of the dominator.

The presentation of the new world, America, in the form of a naked woman, is a proclamation of the function of domination, in which, yesterday as today, sexuality is a key element.

The European allegory clearly expresses the invader's awareness that, in order to subjugate Latin America, he must first "tame" her sexually. On an unconscious level, this attitude expresses simply the underlying male fear of the unknown—an unknown represented so profoundly in the female biological process, especially motherhood, universally symbolized in soil and fertility. Here, woman is the secret dominator. Man is her subject. America is to Europe as the female to the male.

The same image recalls that woman's body is the locus of sexual domination. Hence the special urgency of her subjugation and domestication. Furthermore, sexuality is not autonomous. It is not a world apart from the world of politico-cultural and economico-social domination.

Capitalist Bulwark: Puritanical Sexual Domination

Our Latin American historical experience demonstrates that sexuality is not an individual problem. It is a complex social and cultural reality. It maintains relationships with the prevailing economic system. A study of feminine Latin American religious process cannot be divorced from an analysis of European efforts, throughout the colonial process, to domesticate sexuality.

Of special importance in this process is the puritanical current in Christianity, championed by religious reformers in the sixteenth century. Puritanism dovetailed perfectly with the capitalist mode of production, which, like Victorian puritanism, reached the peak of its maturity in the nineteenth century.

Puritanism coincided with the sexual ideology of the biblical sexual tradition, with its adventitious elements of Stoicism and Neoplatonism later reinforced by the moralistic rigorism of a William of Occam and the seventeenth-century Catholic Jansenist enlightenment.

Otto Maduro has shown that this rigoristic outlook conceives sexuality essentially as an evil energy, to be either repressed or orientated exclusively to the propagation of the species. It likewise coincides with a view of sexuality as an individual dimension, isolated from the rest of the personality.[3]

Thus viewed, sexuality seemed to have no connection with either economics or politics or anything else in history—except that it had to be regulated according to the norms laid down by society and church, norms that sacralized the fragmentation and individualization of sexuality.

Christian puritanism installed sexuality at the center of its official pastoral ministry and practice, thus seeking to polarize the personal and collective energy of the faithful. In the pastoral activity of the Catholic Church since the sixteenth century, sexual morality has moved from the peripheral, secondary status it had in the Middle Ages with an Albertus Magnus or a Thomas Aquinas, to constitute for all practical purposes the principal focus of that activity. The resultant polarization of sexual morality has meant the relegation of politico-social concerns to a secondary status. Hence we have the tendency, since that time, to identify "sin" all but exclusively with a particular sort of sexual behavior.

This chronological process has coincided with the initiation and development of the evangelization of Latin America and the worldwide expansion of capitalism. Its contribution to the support of the capitalist system is based on two main factors:

1. It is the vehicle of a conception of sexuality that reduces the human body to a means of the social production of surplus value,

thereby reinforcing capitalism's natural tendency to exploit the human being as the basic labor force of social relationships of production.

The human body is not only the primary, indispensable material basis of a society's existence, but also the primary, indispensable means and principal element of social production.

2. Inasmuch as evil is now most easily found in sexuality, it is no longer necessary to judge the social structure in moral terms. Or at best, that structure will be judged as a lesser evil. Individuals should bend their greatest efforts to overcome sin, which, in the prevailing view of sexuality, is now almost entirely an individual concern, hence no longer a subject for examination in terms of social relationships. Nor is there any longer any reason for the faithful to direct their attention and energy toward the struggle against human beings' exploitation of one another, which for that matter is no longer the greatest sin, but a minor sin.

This outlook had another consequence, one of a socio-cultural order. It bolstered the ideology of male supremacy and a cultural model according to which all personal energy ought to be focused on the construction and reproduction of intrafamilial relationships rather than being expended in the area of socio-political action.

A male-supremacist capitalism has tended to impose on women of the various social classes the ideal of a total concentration of their energy on intrafamiliar relationships. But the male ought to dedicate only a part of his time to these relationships, the part left over from the production of surplus value.

Thus woman appears as more religious, more family-oriented, less political, less professional. However, this is not due to the nature of the feminine. Nor is it owing to chance. It is due to the historico-social subjugation of women, as reinforced by the view of sexuality propagated by a rigoristic, puritanical Christianity.

We must emphasize that the marginalization of woman from all public life has been carried forward in two ways. First, she has been regarded as a minor, scarcely more than an imbecile. Thus she must be placed under tutelage and guardianship. Secondly, she has been exalted, by a kind of sublimation that renders activities outside the home somehow beneath her dignity. And so the only two vocations available to woman since the nineteenth century have been motherhood and consecrated virginity.

This has had another basic consequence, one of a religious nature. It has produced an aberration in Marian devotion—or rather a male-supremacist exploitation of devotion to the Virgin Mary. Mary is the synthesis of both aspects, virginity and motherhood. Thus she symbolizes the traditional ideal of woman (in a male-supremacist reading of her life).

This model of ideal femininity, in the tenor of an exaltation of the virtues regarded as proper to woman—modesty, a resigned acceptance of any and all reality as the will of God—has been of enormous service and satisfaction to males in the maintenance of their position of privilege. At the same time it has continued to demand of woman that she "accept her place" with humility and resignation, and leave the affairs of world and church to man.

This model marked the life of the church up until the middle of the twentieth century.[4]

Woman, Sexuality, and Catholic Action

In the middle of the nineteenth century a series of changes occurred. Although they were centered in the developed countries, they noticeably influenced Latin America, for Latin America implemented all the mid-century liberal reforms and structured itself in function of an internationalized market and political reality.

The politico-social transformations that produced the industrial revolution also influenced family life. A patriarchal society now entered a state of crisis. Women and children were suddenly in the capitalist marketplace as "personnel." Now their bodies were an additional article of merchandise. In the working family, the ideal of woman's place as in the home began to dissolve. The patriarchal family was weakened in certain ways. Various social classes now became the scene of a movement for "women's rights."

The urbanization process, jobs outside the home, access to education, the diffusion of birth control methods, changed family life, and with it the mentality of women's role in society, church, and home.

Certain individual figures—like María Cano, if I may be permitted to cite the example of a Colombian—fought in the political arena and the union movement, encouraging women's participation in these areas, taking advantage of women's presence in factories, and profiting from the dissemination of ideas like those of the socialist, anarchist, or liberal democratic movements.

Women of economic means began the fight for suffrage, matriculation in the universities, and admittance to the affluent and prestigious professions.

The Church's first reaction to the "feminist" onslaught was to reassert the values of the traditional family and the role of woman in the home. The last flutter of this reactionary ecclesiastical movement occurred in the early part of the twentieth century, with the encyclical *Casti Connubii* (1931).

But historical development cannot be restrained by declarations, and the Church itself had to adapt to the new reality. This is a fundamental moment in its history. In order to perform its activity the church now had to avail itself of the weapons of its adversaries. And so lay organizations, rather like political parties, sprang into being. Now large masses of the Christian people could be encouraged to move toward the same ideological ends.

These permanent organizations of "militant Catholics" or Catholic activists eventually became a genuine mass movement. Antonio Gramsci regards them as a genuine church party. Their function was to provide the framework in which the Catholic masses could be used as a weapon—offensive or defensive as exigencies of the political, social, and especially cultural struggle might require.

The laity, male and female, was issued a call to participate in the apostolate of the hierarchy. Women took up the Catholic Action experiment, then in its infancy, and mounted a struggle for a place in evangelization and the pastoral ministry, the core of the life of the church. Woman had begun to emerge from her traditional role of wife in the home and consecrated virgin in the religious community.

Nevertheless, she was required to reinforce the traditional view of sexuality. To this end, she was kept in a sexless state, a kind of childlike innocence, instead of being helped to assume her sexual reality as woman.

The young unmarried women of Catholic Action were entrusted with forming leagues and conducting campaigns for moral behavior and good habits. The accent was on maximal control of the media (film, radio), amusement, and recreation. A great deal of insistence was placed on a rigoristic morality that eschewed flirting, dancing, the theater, novels, sports, and summer relaxation. The traditional view of sexuality as the capital sin, and woman as a near occasion of sin, prevailed.

This was the attitude adopted by the lay associations, pastors, bishops, and the Vatican itself, in the problem of women's dress. As woman's body was the supreme occasion of sin, it was important that it be covered as completely as possible. The model dress for the Catholic Action girl in our tropical countries consisted in high collars, long gray skirts reaching halfway from the knee and the ankle, thus hiding the legs, high button shoes, loose sleeves, and a sombrero!

Women's morality leagues exerted a great influence on Latin American cultural life, especially among young unmarried women, and especially in the middle and upper classes. Their moralistic outlook was accepted by all Catholic movements. More than ever before, celibacy was presented as the only model of holiness. Marriage was an inferior calling. Small wonder, then, that to militant Catholics the only true avenue to holiness seemed to be the religious life.[5]

The religious life was a reaction to the historical transformations set afoot by the massive presence of women in the factories at the turn of the century. Women cut their braids. They exchanged their long, heavy nineteenth-century clothing for short, light dresses. They emerged from the vigilance of their families into the new demands of their condition as paid laborers, with the freedom and independence of wage earners, and they adapted to these demands. Their attitude toward their bodies began to change. So did their carriage. They began to alter their world of affective relationships. New sexual conduct appeared.[6]

Like the rest of the population, nearly all Catholics hoped somehow to remain in the past. And so leagues of "decency" and morality were founded, constituted of the young ladies of Catholic Action, directed by the clergy, and functioning as guardians of feminine modesty.

But toward the end of the 1940s, certain young women joined the university student movement, especially in Chile and Brazil. In 1947 the Chilean Catholic Student Movement sent Olga de Cruz Grez to Potoise, in France, for the Second Conference of the JEC (Catholic Student Youth) International. In 1953 Maria de Lourdes

Figuereido, of Brazil, participated in an international meeting of Pax Romana in Denmark, where she was elected vice-president of that worldwide organization—the first Latin American to hold office at the international level in an organization of Catholic students.

Beginning in 1950, due to the presence of women in the universities, all the Latin American movements gradually integrated. The old male and female branches of Catholic Action, composed almost entirely of university students, now joined forces. It was originally intended to have two presidents, so as to guarantee a female presence at the top level. This custom was abolished in many countries almost at once. But Gustavo Gutiérrez, then a young university chaplain in Peru, always insisted on the importance of respecting the female contribution to the organization by maintaining a female presence among the national officers.[7]

Students began to take their distance from the traditional Catholic Action outlook on sexuality. They sought to acquire a solid moral formation that would permit youth to live their sexuality with a genuine freedom and maturity. But sex, and male-female relationships—and still less the condition of women in society and the church—were never central to their discussions.

Women and the Birth of the Theology of Liberation

Thus a rigoristic, puritanical outlook on sexuality prevailed in Latin America in some form or other until the great upheavals of the 1960s. Then, amid such changes in the life of the Church, and of our continent, we discovered that if we were to live in a genuine Christianity, we should have to become involved in the construction and liberation of Latin America.

To this end it was considered essential to overcome our underdevelopment. Here the key points were agrarian reform, an autonomous capitalism, and a breach of our colonial ties—political, economic, and cultural—with the developed metropolises.

This posture was then influenced by the Cuban revolution, the dialogue between Christianity and Marxism, the political struggle of priests like Camilo Torres, the partial breakdown of the Christian Democratic parties, and the contribution of the developing social sciences.

The experience constituted a break with the spirituality of the age. Latin American Catholic youth now based their religious experience on the so-called Jocist methodology (JOC—Jeunesse Ouvrière Catholique): the *révision de vie.* Now the watchword was "to see, to judge, to act." Now our basic thrust, whether we were girls or boys, was an attempt to embody the gospel, the sacramental life, and prayer, in our own young lives through the witness we could give in the factories, at the universities, on the farm, and in our families. In the church itself, we became engaged in a struggle for the freedom and the rights of the laity, male and female, with a view to being able to act on society in the way that seemed correct to us as Christians.

It was in the youth movements of the 1960s, then, that young women and men joined forces to pass a point of no return. The movement we launched of course had ample theoretical support, in the teaching of Vatican II. In practice, however, at least in Latin America, we could not depend on adequate support on the part of the bishops, and some years later our experiment was crushed by one sector of the episcopate.

We had found a new way of being Christian. But its authenticity was misunderstood by the majority of the clergy, and our movement had no church support. And so, in the 1970s, except in Peru and a few dioceses in the rest of Latin America, we were made to toe the line; or else our movements were watered down into political groups, so that they lost their effectiveness as a church experiment. Still, the religious lives of young persons, male and female, had been renewed, and a church committed to the popular sectors would be reborn.

It is to this Catholic youth experiment in Latin America that Gustavo Gutiérrez refers in the opening lines of his *Teología de la liberación* (1971):

> This book is an attempt at reflection, based on the Gospel and *the experiences of men and women committed to the process of liberation* in the oppressed and exploited land of Latin America. It is a theological reflection born of the experience of shared efforts to abolish the current unjust situation and to build a different society, freer and more human. Many in Latin America have started along the path of a commitment to lib-

> eration, and among them is a growing number of Christians; whatever the validity of these pages, it is due to their experiences and reflections. My greatest desire is not to betray their experiences and efforts to elucidate the meaning of their solidarity with the oppressed.
>
> My purpose is not to elaborate an ideology to justify postures already taken, nor to undertake a feverish search for security in the face of the radical challenges which confront the faith, nor to fashion a theology from which political action is "deduced." It is rather to let ourselves be judged by the word of the Lord, to think through our faith, to strengthen our love, and to give reason for our hope from within a commitment that seeks to become more radical, total, and efficacious. It is to reconsider the great themes of the Christian life within this radically changed perspective and with regard to the new questions posed by this commitment. This is the goal of the so-called *theology of liberation.*[8]

At the same time as this effort was being carried forward by the Catholic Action youth of the 1960s, religious communities, especially those of women, were keeping pace, in their own work with the popular sectors. In communities with both a female and a male branch, like Maryknoll, it was frequently the sisters who more quickly intuited and understood what it meant to live the faith in a commitment of solidarity with the oppressed.

The students who had "been to the barrios" were unable to continue their labors of "conscientization" and evangelization. But women religious, especially, and some priests, who had understood the message of the Christian youth of the 1960s, took up the relays, and it was they who laid the foundation for a church of communion and participation in the following decade.

Priests who had been chaplains in the Latin American movements, along with certain bishops who had encouraged these same movements, were inspired to organize small communities and use the youth methodology to launch the comprehensive pastoral ministry proposed in the Medellín Final Document (Second Conference of the Latin American Episcopate, 1968).

In the 1970s certain sectors of the church, taking their cue from the documents of the Medellín Conference, as well as from their experience of a church that sought before all else to be the servant of the people, concentrated their efforts on creating base or grass-roots communities. The membership and influence of these sectors grew, and it was on the basis of the reflections issuing from the communities they founded that they continued to develop the major themes of the theology of liberation.

The enormous contribution of Catholic Action youth to the history of the Latin American Church is frequently ignored. It is said that this was only the work of a few elitist minorities. But as Pablo Richard states, to effect a sociological reduction of, and give a merely sociological significance to, theological reality is to forget the many little minorities in the history of the church who made a critical interpretation of history and the will of God, and communicated the result to broader communities.

I should like to emphasize that, just as men and women joined hands to make their commitment to the cause of liberation, so also both sexes were able to share all responsibilities involved. Their shared experience, together with the general social and cultural transformations underway, taught men—chaplains and lay militants—that women have a right to a place in society and the church not as minors, or indeed as children without the use of reason, but on an equal footing with men. Men learned that women, too, have a right to make decisions. However, there was still a long way to go. We women were entrusted with responsibilities, but, unconsciously, we were required to abandon our female identity. Anyone embracing the feminist theory, then being developed among European and North American women, was put in her place with the allegation that feminism was an imperialist theory calculated to divide and weaken the popular sector.

Those of us who were part of these movements, who were working for a transformation of society, saw the need to change woman's situation in society and in the church as part of that transformation. But we strove in this direction by our actions, not by discussion. We were certainly not about to proclaim ourselves feminists, if that was what feminists were accused of. Besides, feminism was seen as an antimale movement. Finally, and especially, as good Catholics we had internalized the ideology of abnegation and resignation to the point where it would have seemed altogether too forward, and hence morally wrong, to make any claims in our own behalf.

And because we had to perform our activity in a society like the church—an essentially male-dominated society, with a patriarchal ideology, accustomed to relegate women to subordinate functions—we had to, if I may say so, practically disguise ourselves as men. We had to reason like men, act with the same combativeness as men, use men's vocabulary, and live a man's spirituality. In a word, we had to become male, or at least present ourselves as asexual beings.

This was also the framework in which the theology of liberation came into being. Obviously, then, that theology was not going to address the situation of women in the Church and society. Nor would it concern itself with the male-female relationship. Indeed, in a first moment, liberation theology was unconcerned to deal with the moral theology of sex.

I must say, however, that some community chaplains did insist on the need to take account of the feminine perspective and the importance of women's active participation in decision-making in the life of the Church. Gustavo Gutiérrez is a particularly admirable case in point. Although he did not include the topic in his *A Theology of Liberation,* he was utterly aware of women's participation in the experiences he is systematizing. As we have seen, he explicitly states in his introduction that these experiences are those "of men and women."

In a second moment—when liberation theology had become a product of the systematization of a Christian experience immersed in popular reality—although religious women had been the first to intuit and assume this radically new way of being Christian, once again it was clerical males who wrote the books. Only one liberation theologian, Leonardo Boff, dealt with the subject directly, in his *The Maternal Face of God* (1979).[9]

Today, within the Church itself, a battle is being waged for a new male-female relationship. Very timidly, a feminist theology is being sketched within the current of liberation theology, incorporating elements of feminist theory and today's moral theology.

An ever-growing group of women, lay and religious, in Latin

America today is doing theology, and related disciplines like religious sociology or church history, from the same perspective, seeking to consolidate, within the popular movement in the Church, a new kind of man-woman relationship.

In Quest of New Horizons

The Latin American Church has made a commitment to the quest for liberation. Therefore it is posing the question of sexuality. At the base, grassroots level, that church acknowledges the need to review and correct woman's position in the church and society. This need is felt in the hearts of men and women who experience the painful sexual unidimensionality of our society and our church. How could they not react?

Accordingly, I hold the urgency of (1) a review of the puritanical conception of sexuality as the ideological foundation, in the Church as in Latin American society, of the patriarchal mentality on which all sexist oppression is based; (2) a prophetic denunciation of the process of feminization of poverty as the product of the capitalist system and of racism; and (3) a contribution on the part of Latin American women, and from our own female viewpoint, to the recovery of the liberating strength of Jesus and Mary.

Toward a Human, Christian Concept of Sexuality

We Latin American men and women have been calling for the actualization of a dimension that has always existed in Christianity, but which in the last centuries, for the reasons stated above, has been forgotten: human sexuality is something willed by God. It is God who created humanity sexed. Sexuality is a gift of God.

My outlook is traditional, then, and central to the Christian view of creation. And yet it has been forgotten. As we have seen, its place has been usurped by the tendency to regard believers who live their sexuality as somehow unfit for the divine life. This attitude is not the original Christian one. In fact, it has been reinforced by philosophical propositions alien to Christianity, such as Stoicism, Neoplatonism, and Victorian puritanism.

The concept of sexuality as something that estranges its subject from God, and hence something to be repressed, has not only motivated a repressive pastoral theory and practice, as we have seen, but has proposed asexuality as the only viable model of a Christian lifestyle and a monastic spirituality as the Christian ideal.

Today the only way to begin is to break with the traditional notion that reduces sexuality to an isolated area of the social relationship and an expression of sin, the latter being embodied essentially in woman.

It must be recognized that religious experience is neither essentially masculine, nor essentially feminine, nor essentially asexual. It is simply and fully a human experience. We must acknowledge that each of the sexes constitutes a way by which the human being reaches self-expression. Human beings achieve reality only as sexual beings, and they must be enabled to do this in all fullness, and in the possession of their rights. There are two ways of achieving this realization, then, and each of the two ways must be permitted to retain its originality through the adoption of continually new formulas.

Indeed, we have come to grasp that sexuality can contain a special experience of spirituality, or the encounter with God. Sexuality is expressed in love for one's partner, one's "con-sort"—the person with whom one shares a common lot. But the experience of God comes precisely by way of such an encounter with the "other," one's neighbor. Spirituality is a specific manner of self-encounter, of self-discovery, of the search for unification and oneness. In the love expressed in conjugal life, in the sexual life, appears the total, comprehensive encounter of two beings who give themselves up to one another fully and reciprocally. Here is a unique, privileged experience of horizons of transcendence. In sexuality, then, lived as the expression of love, we may find—have a living experience of—God.[10]

However, we shall not have this living experience, this empirical adventure, without a battle for the liberation of woman. That struggle cannot be separated from the struggle for the full realization of the human being. The former is a part of the latter. No wonder we men and women find it difficult to begin a journey whose starting point is a breach with the traditional notion of sexuality. But only thus can we begin the journey to a genuinely comprehensive liberation.

The Feminization of Poverty in the Modern World

Jesus criticized "stubbornness"—hardheartedness and thick-headedness. It is with this same thickheadedness that we conjure up an anthropological and sexual inequality between the women and men. Our sexual division of labor is dehumanizing for both.

Woman has traditionally been entrusted with the tasks of hearth and home. Then that assignment has been belittled in comparison with the task of culture-building traditionally preempted by man.

Feminist studies have called attention to the worldwide process of the feminization of poverty. In 1980 the United Nations Organization reported:

1. Women constitute one-half of the world population.
2. Women spend twice as much time at work as men do.
3. They receive one-tenth of the world's income.
4. They possess less than one percent of the world's wealth.

This impoverishment of women is due in part to notions of motherhood, and to discrimination with regard to work and wages. That is, the feminization of poverty is a consequence of sexism (especially of sexist notions of economic processes) complemented by racial oppression.[11]

Racial discrimination, sexism, and capitalist exploitation in Latin America constitute the triad that keeps women in subjection. Latin Americans who dismiss feminism as a "bourgeois issue" are altogether off the mark. On the contrary, one of the basic tasks incumbent on Christians is to struggle against *all* discrimination—social, racial, and sexual.

Recapturing the Liberating Strength of Jesus and Mary

The life of Jesus is the Christian model par excellence. And so we women of Latin America never tire of reminding the community that Jesus' attitude toward women was never discriminatory, however radical a break with the traditions of his time he saw this to be. The figure of Mary—Mary poor, Mary committed and engaged—so central to our Latin American piety, is for us the power and model of liberation as the process of the feminization of poverty waxes apace.

Without having to use any rhetoric—but overturning, subverting the social order of his time—Jesus accorded all values, rights, and opportunities to all women of his time. In manifesting this humane attitude, he furnished us with a new model for the man-woman relationship.

From the first day of creation, God's plan has included the equality of man and woman. Both, male and female, are God's image. The image of God is that of mother-and-father. God is the synthesis of a sexed humanity:

> God created humankind in God's image;
> in the divine image God created them;
> male and female God created them.
> God blessed them, saying: "Be fertile and multiply;
> fill the earth and subdue it" [Gen. 1:27–28].

God, our Father and Mother, blessed the creature, and entrusted it, male and female, with one and the same mission: together, to be fertile and multiply and fill the earth and subject it to themselves jointly. That is, we are both responsible for the co-creation of home and society. Both of us, man and woman.

Today, in a culture and society of concrete challenges that tend to recast the role of woman and man in home and society, we face fears, perplexities, and anxieties. We have set aside the divine command. We have refused to accept the equality of man and woman, who, in complementarity, constitute the image of God, and to whom God gave the common task of filling and subduing the earth.

Jesus had to recall this to persons of his time when he spoke of the question of divorce:

> [Moses] wrote that commandment [permitting divorce] for you because of your stubbornness. At the beginning of creation God made them male and female [Mark 10:5–6].

And still today our stubbornness and hardheartedness refuse to allow us to recall this absolutely basic fact: that from the beginning of creation God has made us male and female.

When we see woman's ability and maturity in undertaking the construction of society and culture (without abandoning her post in the home), we are awestruck. Women themselves are surprised at the breadth of their creative capacities. We forget that this is simply God's plan. It always has been.

We also forget that it is only the dynamics of the human historical process that have produced a society of male domination. What pertains to historical contingency is not carved in stone. It can be changed. By no manner of means must we allow it to be dogmatized. On the contrary, we must recover the attitude that the humanity God created is one, and that it is sexual.

Jesus calls women to set off down the road of their own liberation. After all, he has incorporated them into his church. There is no question of "feminism" in the sense of an insurrection in the cause of freedom. What is asked of us—men and women alike—is that we adopt a view, an outlook, that acknowledges the existence and condition of women. The advancement of women is only a particular aspect of the good news that Jesus proclaims to the poor, the privileged object of his liberation.

Those Jesus calls to build his reign are in the first instance the disinherited, the marginalized, the excluded. Among them are women, children, pagans, and sinners. Jesus prefers them because he discovers unknown, neglected values in them. It is a simple fact, attested by all four gospels, that the good news of Jesus includes women in the community called to build his reign.

We Latin Americans are becoming daily more conscious of the urgency of integrating the fight for women's rights into the struggle for the rights of society's other marginalized. We are not mounting a separate movement. Ours is but part of the one battle for a society of fellowship in which we can live the love of Jesus. The building of the reign is an affair of men and women together. Only united are we God's likeness and expression. But given the situation of women's historical oppression, it becomes absolutely necessary to accord a special interest to their advancement as part of the process of comprehensive liberation. Only thus—by incorporating women into the liberative struggle of the continent—shall we succeed in building a genuinely human society of brothers and sisters.

Mary in the Christian Community: Model of Liberation

Mary has been held out to Christians as a model of the feminine. But like the image of Jesus, so also that of Mary has frequently been utilized to justify a patriarchal mentality that marginalizes women. Mary has been simplified. She has become the model of self-denial, passivity, and submission as the essential (or worse still, the only) attributes of woman.

We are altogether accustomed to this predominantly patriarchal discourse. Despite efforts like those of Paul VI in *Marialis Cultus*, or of Puebla, Mary's genuine quality does not "come through" sufficiently to rescue the whole prophetic, liberative dimension that her mystery can offer the Latin American woman and man of today.

Jesus not only reminds us insistently that the female human being is God's daughter as much as the male is God's son. He not only incorporates this daughter of his into his church. He not only values her pedagogy highly enough to summon the people of God to hear her word and experience her prophetic role of proclamation. He actually takes a woman and makes her his mother, to fulfill God's plan by taking flesh within her.

From our Latin American viewpoint, the figure of the mother of Jesus helps us rediscover the role of woman and man, and calls us to be converted and sanctified by accepting her liberative dimension.

Luke 1:26–33 teaches us that the humility of Mary consists in the daring to accept the monumental undertaking proposed to her by God. At first Mary is in wonder. She is unsettled and disturbed, as a woman, at what God proposes to her. But the angel promises that the shadow of the Spirit will cover her. Then Mary says: "I am the servant of the Lord. Let it be done to me as you say" (Luke 1:38).

Mary's yes is a free, responsible yes by which she accepts being the vessel of the new creation to be embodied by her son Jesus. It is not the yes of self-denial, almost of irresponsibility, as it has been traditionally presented to us. Mary knows to whom she is committing herself.

We women of contemporary society, in all freedom, responsibility, and availability, hereby accept God's invitation to be part of the Church that is to carry out the new evangelization. We accept God's invitation to share in the building of the new society.

We understand Mary's submission as a free act of surrender and self-bestowal for the purpose of co-creating, together with us, a new kind of humanistic and humanizing culture—one that will permit us to deliver ourselves from the rationalistic, inhumane, dehumanizing, hence discriminatory and utilitarian, culture of domination around us.

Like Mary, who receives God's invitation and accepts it freely and responsibly, so that the Spirit covers her and she becomes a servant "according to the word" ("according to your word" being the Greek idiom for the "as you say" of Luke 1:38), we accept the challenge of the third Christian millennium.

Mary is blessed because she bears and communicates life even though she knows the suffering her son will undergo in pursuit of the liberation of his people. What a blessing for our faith that she believed! Mary, a woman, is the model disciple for Latin American men and women performing the joint task of giving birth to a new society.

In a society like ours in Latin America, which has denied us the right to motherhood by sterilizing us psychologically (through the radical birth control campaigns) and economically (on a continent drowning in foreign debt)—where, politically, we are denied the right to life because dissent is silenced with prison, torture, and the threat of being put on a death list—where those who do their duty are murdered—where the use and abuse of drugs in the United States and the drug traffic in Latin America is killing our children, husbands, brothers, and friends—Mary, the prophet of the Magnificat, gives us the strength to fight, in solidarity and in community, for the right to life.

Mary's song sustains us in our quest for a bright tomorrow for our Latin American children. After all, her song proclaims to us that the promise is being fulfilled—that liberation, by God's mercy, is at hand:

> He has shown might with his arm;
> he has confused the proud in their inmost thoughts.
> He has deposed the mighty from their thrones
> and raised the lowly to high places.
> The hungry he has given every good thing,
> while the rich he has sent empty away [Luke 1:51–53].

Mary the lowly servant of God—woman Mary—is God's decree of liberation, and the model of our action today. Woman—Latin

American mother, eternal Eve, everlasting communicator of life—is also, like Mary, ever the first to communicate the good news, and thus to engender in her offspring a sense and feeling for their own life. The figure of Mother Mary helps us re-create woman's role, her identity and sense of belonging in the world. Man alone cannot create that world.

In today's world of sorrow and suffering, despair, war, and violence, where technological and scientific progress threaten to cancel life, the task of Latin American woman is to advocate, foster, further, and assume a commitment to the building of the new society and the new evangelization, so that she may never cease to give birth.

For now, she shares this dimension in precious few sectors of the Latin American Church community. But little by little, she is coming into her own in the ministry and pastoral theology of the base communities. Feminist theology has called attention to the fact that the traditional oppression of women continues to be maintained among us at all levels of society, and that one of the great sins of the Church is to have sacralized this oppression through its patriarchal discourse and the attitude of the majority of its leaders.

It is therefore incumbent upon us as Christian men and women to seek the genuine liberation of our peoples. It is our task to initiate a project that will permit the popular sectors (1) to assimilate Latin American history and the lot of women in that history, that by understanding our past we may understand our present and be able to transform it, building a genuinely human future; (2) to develop the capacity to submit to judgment by the word of the Lord, that we may make an irrevocable commitment to the building of the reign of God—the genuine reign of God, made up of male and female.

2

Women Doing Theology in Latin America

Ivone Gebara

The expression "women doing theology" is new, as is the explication of what the expression means. Previously, there was never any mention of sexual difference with regard to those who wrote theology, since it was obvious that the task was something proper to men. Today it would seem that the matter is no longer obvious, and the gender of the authors must be specified. Gender is understood not only as a biological difference prior even to birth, but especially as a cultural dimension, that is, as a stance or an aspect that affects the production of other cultural values, of other kinds of human interrelationship and other ways of thinking.

The fact that women have entered the world of economic production and, more broadly, into politics and culture and the consequences for change in society and in the various churches deserves deeper reflection on its own. Such a deepening would go beyond the scope of our contribution, since right now we have another aim.

I am going to devote my attention especially to the question of the task of theology, emphasizing some points of reflection on what

---

Translated from Portuguese by Phillip Berryman.

has already been said, and I shall continue my reflection beyond issues that are properly theological.

What Characterizes the Way Women Do Theology?

In order to sketch a response to this question, we must first explain what we understand today by the theological activity of women. I should make it clear that my starting point is the situation in northeastern Brazil. Placing myself at that starting point is crucially important, since it conditions my reflection as a woman out of a particular socioeconomic, political, and cultural situation. This situation shapes my being and my acting, my seeing and my feeling, my speech and my silence.

To speak or write from northeast Brazil is to situate myself in a region where misery and exploitation take on extremely dehumanizing forms and where most of the people, and especially women, are its victims. This region is the victim of internal and external contradictions of the capitalist system and is marked by various kinds of contrasts: *(a)* by economic and social contrasts: a few large-scale property-owners, most people landless, very high unemployment; *(b)* by political contrasts: power of the "colonels"—sugar-mill owners, industrialists, and politicians—alongside the lack of decision-making power on the part of millions of people in the northeast; *(c)* by cultural contrasts: utilization of popular culture to serve the dominant culture, machismo, and subjection of women.

As we know well, these contrasts entail enormous social consequences, reducing most of the people to subhuman living conditions. It is out of this situation, which sustains my being and my reflection, that I can speak of women's theology. I recognize that I am a woman who lives in privileged conditions, conditions that give me enough space to reflect, to speak, and even to write. I speak of the woman that I am myself, and of others, the poor women of my region, in an effort to move over into their world on the basis of my option for our liberation, as well as on the basis of our common human condition as women.

As I see it, the theological task is multiple and varied. There is nothing new about such a statement. What may be new is the fact of explicating it from the starting point of the situation of women. Hence, I speak of different theological tasks.

Shared Experiences

There is a way of doing theology that starts with shared experience from oral transmission, from the simple fact of sharing life. I believe this way of doing theology is what is most representative of the popular milieus. Many women are especially gifted with a deep intuition about human life and are able to counsel, to intuit problems, to express them, to give support, to propose solutions, and to confirm the faith of many people. They explain biblical passages on the basis of their experience and respond to doctrinal questions by simplifying them and setting them on the level of existential reality. Some of these women are illiterate. That would pose problems for a more academic doing of theology, but it does not hinder the exercise of this ministry. This activity is sapiential; it springs from life, and life is its reference point. It is received as a gift from God and handed on as a gift.

Discourse dealing with the important issues in life is the heart of every theology. God's life is related to the life of humankind, and the life of humankind is related to God. All subsequent systematizing, all thematizing, all connecting of ideas, is vitally linked to this most basic aspect.

With regard to this primordial religious experience, it is important that we take note of the function of women in Candomblé,* especially in northeast Brazil. I draw attention to this point simply to underscore the fact that even in machistic cultures like our own, in Camdomblé the woman has a special place in carrying out religious tasks. The "Mother of the Saint" is "queen" in her own territory. She is the recipient of the wish of the saint, male or female; she transmits or presides over and coordinates religious ceremonies. Generally speaking, this sort of thing does not take place in Christian churches, although one can cite some similar nonofficial functions: counselors, prayer leaders, faith healers, and providers of other services deeply connected to the religious dimension of human life. In some Protestant churches, female priestly ministry

*"Candomblé" is an Afro-Brazilian religious ceremony composed of prayers, dances, and offerings led by a priest (Padre Santo) or a priestess (Madre del Santo) with the purpose of invoking the good spirits and expelling the bad ones.

is allowed, but it is not exercised at all among the popular sectors in northeast Brazil.

Efforts of Popular Catechists

The theological efforts of the so-called popular catechists, who are responsible for more systematic initiation into Christian doctrine, especially among children and young people, can be one of repeating written materials, things learned in their own childhood, or ideas imposed by priests. One can also find a dimension of impressive creativity, which has a strong influence on the life of children and young people. Today in Latin America one can speak of a "revolutionary role" played by many catechists who open themselves clearly and effectively to the problems of their people and who have shown that they can both take an active role in popular movements and pass on to children and young people a Christianity characterized by the struggle for justice, a high value placed on life, and the sharing of goods. In so doing, they provide alternatives to this consumerist and individualistic society.

Catholic Sisters

The theological effort of Catholic sisters among the popular sectors is a kind of work that became significant in Brazil, especially during the 1970s. The "migration" of sisters to popular milieus, and the fact that young people in those areas have taken on religious life while remaining to serve in those milieus, have strengthened and continue to strengthen a consciousness and militancy in the popular organizations as well as a reading of Christian faith whose starting point is the problems and hopes of our people.

The presence of these sisters has stimulated and motivated a rereading of the Bible as the history of a people to whom we are linked by religious tradition and from whom we must learn fidelity to life, and in particular fidelity to a book that tells us about Jesus and Mary, figures who set in motion a new way for people to relate to one another.

Something new is happening in the people's theological expression. There seems to be a before and an after, that is, the presence of these sisters often seems to establish the context that enables the poor to experience certain elements of change in the way they formulate and live their religion. The image of a God committed to the liberation of the poor, of a Mary closer to women's problems, of a Jesus who is less remote and whose words are understandable in our own situation—these are just examples of the enormous change that gradually takes place.

Doing Theology from Daily Life

The theological activity of women who teach in theology departments and institutes is a ministry not limited just to courses but involves advising the various groups and movements in the Christian churches. Above and beyond the academic theological formation, which both men and women receive in higher institutions of learning where men are the majority, there is something quite special in the way that women do theology. The elements of everyday life are very intertwined with their speaking about God. When women's experience is expressed in a church whose tradition is machistic, the other side of human experience returns to theological discourse: the side of the person who gives birth, nurses, nourishes, of the person who for centuries has remained silent with regard to anything having to do with theology. Now she begins to express her experience of God, in another manner, a manner that does not demand that reason alone be regarded as the single and universal mediation of theological discourse. This way of doing theology includes what is vital, utilizing mediations that can help to express what has been experienced, without exhausting it, a discourse that leads to the awareness that there is always something more, something that words cannot express.

What is vital cannot be expressed through formal mediations. It can be done only through those mediations that are proper to a sapiential discourse in which relationships with others express the diversity and complexity of human situations and challenges. Theological speech is expressed in the kind of prophecy that denounces the present, in songs of hope, in lament, in the form of counsel. It is as though the aim were to bridge the gap between speech and reality, the distance that the formal and idealist discourse of religion has imposed on us for a long time. It is as though we were discovering, very powerfully and starting from our own situation, the mystery of the incarnation of the divine in the human, not just because "we have been told," but because we experience it in the confines of our lives as women.

The experience of this theological activity is still in its early stages. In Brazil there are not many published works to confirm it and make it known. There is only what I regard as most basic and prior to theological elaboration: faith and its expression based on an encounter with the experience of the oppression of women as an experience of the oppression of the poor. This expression has been more oral and more direct, and has proved to be effective.

At this point, I am limiting myself to taking note of this kind of activity. Further on, I shall seek to explain some characteristics, intuitions, and efforts involved in this activity.

Historic Contexts

The different theological activities spelled out above take place on different levels and in different situations, characterized by various kinds of conditionings. At this point, I propose that we reflect on some "historic contexts" and some characteristics that, I think, are proper to women doing theology in Latin America during these last few years. The basis on which I point to these contexts and their characteristics is my own observation and the way I exercise this ministry, which is confirmed by the practice of a few of my colleagues and by the reception given by the audience I address.

I cannot avoid speaking about my own experience. In a vital way it makes me what I am. My theological experience is the product of my relationship with people, of mutual influences, of my philosophical and ideological stance, situated in time and space. The faith I have received from my childhood onward, the difficult and twisting path of my life, the discoveries I have made, the past and the present, have all left their mark on my experience of theology.

It is hard to draw a line between the subjective and the objective, or a line between what I say about others and what I say about myself. In life, such things are mixed together and interconnected, and we risk killing something vital within them if we try to "divide the waters" too precisely. Every "theory" includes something very personal, something deeply involved with the one who elaborates it, something that is part of the very desire to know and change the world. To speak either as a single person or universally seems to show or reflect something that we experience in the everyday reality of our life within our different social and cultural conditionings: the partial nature of our perception and the partial nature of our interpretations.

Thus it is within the boundaries of my subjectivity/objectivity and within the limits of my experience and observation that I set forth the following three historic contexts and three characteristics.

Irruption of History into Women's Lives

When we speak of the irruption of history into the lives of women—and especially the theological expression of their faith—we do not mean the entrance of women into history; they have always been present. What we have in mind is something qualitatively different and new, that is, the irruption of historic consciousness into the lives of millions and millions of women, leading them to the liberation struggle by means of an active participation in different fronts from which they had previously been absent. It is as though a strong wind had begun to blow, opening eyes and loosening tongues, shifting stances, enabling arms to reach out to new embraces and hands to take up other tools, impelling feet to take other steps, raising the voice so its song and its lament might be heard. Woman begins to take her place as agent of history. The fact is that with her activity and new stance toward what happens in life, a new awareness is clearly coming into being. Participation in labor unions, neighborhood movements, mothers' groups, and pastoral leadership all manifest a change in the consciousness and in the role women play today. Entering into history in fact means becoming aware of history, entering into a broader meaning, in which women are also creators or increasingly want to be forgers of history.

Discovering Causality within Women's Experience

In connection with history, one can speak of the causality of things. The condition of women is the result of an evolution: it has been different, and it can be different. Their present state can be partly explained on the basis of historic causes. The discovery of the causes of the oppression of the poor and, among them, of the oppression of women, has changed women's understanding of themselves as persons individually and corporately. Woman is not marked for an unchangeable fate, nor is she the object of alien wills that shape her existence. Despite the conditions inherent in human existence, she can conquer spaces in which to express her word and her being. This new historic moment of hers is pregnant with future, a moment that announces a Good News that is both present and yet to be lived in its fullness.

It is worth noting that the discovery of causality within women's experience bears the characteristic marks of the particular way in which they perceive and approach the problems of life. No one single cause is absolutized but, rather, the causes are multiple. This way of looking at matters is obedient to their perception, as women, in its complexity, diversity, and mystery.

Entering the Labor Force

The fact that more and more women are entering the world of paid labor, and the world of work and struggle for survival, has awakened them to struggle in other areas where human destiny is also at stake.

Entering the labor force has changed the expression of women's faith. From their previous horizon of home and family, women have opened out to a broader reality. God is no longer one who addresses a world limited to the activities of home and family; God becomes the one who addresses socioeconomic and political challenges in the new militancy of Latin American women. The image of God is no longer that of the father to whom one owes submission; rather, God is basically the image of what is most human in woman and man, seeking expression and liberation. A working woman said, "God is the force that won't allow me to surrender to the will of those who oppress my people."

Women's entry into the struggle of the world of paid labor has thus brought about a change in the way they relate. Obviously, this is not the only factor, but it seems important to remind ourselves of it, since it tends to be forgotten or left as a purely accidental aspect within a traditionalist or reactionary theological vision.

Characteristics of Feminist Theological Activity in Latin America

Living Realities and Theological Elaboration

Feminist theological expression always starts from what has been lived, from what is experienced in the present. Consequently it rejects an abstract type of language about life and those matters deeply affecting human relationship. That is why there is a growing effort to clear the field of old theological concepts in order to discover what vital realities they correspond to, and to what extent they really do so. Living realities are the takeoff point for theological elaboration; they are rational symbols that arose in a particular period, the product of a series of conditions, and they were able to bring together rationally certain experiences of reality. It is urgent that we get to know them and discover their meaning for today, and for our history. In their theological work, women seek to retrieve existential realities, to let them speak freely, to allow them to become reorganized on the basis of our context today, and only subsequently to connect them to a prior tradition.

This way of proceeding represents an attempt to restore to theological language its capacity for touching some vital centers of human existence. In other words, to some extent this procedure means returning the poetic dimension of human life to theology, since the deepest meaning in the human being is expressed only through analogy; mystery is voiced only in poetry, and what is gratuitous is expressed only through symbols.

Purely rational concepts do not take into account the meaning, desire, flavor, pleasure, pain, and mystery of existence. Given their own history, women are bolder in questioning concepts, and they have a creative curiosity that opens new paths and allows new understandings. This new mode makes possible a kind of theological creation in community. That is, the new formulation gathers a broader number of experiences and is not narrowed to a formulation or a text with individual "authorship."

This is a "new way" of expressing something after it has been heard, lived, and felt many times and in many ways, so that people recognize themselves when they hear it spelled out, and they feel invited to a deeper reflection on the questions that life poses. It is their own issues that they see reflected on, questioned, or clarified so that the reflection proposed touches most deeply the questions and doubts present in the lives of millions of people.

Re-creating Tradition

In women's theological discourse, the theological tradition shared by the different churches does not function as a legitimizing justification that we need only to go on repeating. If we do repeat, it is because that is what today's situation demands, because it does touch the roots of our existence, because to some extent it responds to the problems that ongoing history sets before us. In this sense, what is normative is primarily the present, what calls out today; tradition is viewed in terms of the present. Thus the tradition of Christian communities in the past is continually re-created, and one may even speak of fidelity to that tradition to the extent that both today and yesterday are faithful to the Spirit of God manifest in history and demanding absolute respect for life. The past is not only information, but enlightenment, teaching, and witness for the present to the extent that it relates to the question of being human.

Human Complexities

The theological work of women reflects an ability to view life as the locus of the simultaneous experience of oppression and liberation, of grace and lack of grace. Such perception encompasses what is plural, what is different, what is other. Although this way of looking is not the exclusive property of women, we must say that it is found to an extraordinary extent among women. In popular struggles, in which women have played a very important role, this ability to grasp in a more unified way the oppositions and contradictions, the contrasts and differences as inherent in human life, has been a characteristic feature of the way in which women live and express their faith. Such behavior enables them to avoid taking dogmatic and exclusive stances, and to perceive or intuit the real complexity of what is human.

The Tapestry of Human Life

In addition to these factors or characteristics of the theological work of women, we cannot fail to recall the inestimable contribution of the social sciences—anthropology, psychology, and different theories about language—as elements that have been changing, directly or indirectly, women's understanding of themselves. These same elements have contributed to the emancipation of women's power in the social dimension of human relations and in the way these relations are organized.

All these contributions form part of the tapestry woven by women expressing and reflecting human life as this century ends. The threads, colors, flowers, and other designs—all taken together, interconnected, and linked to each other—are forming the embroidery of life while the artists themselves are beginning to appear, to show their faces in public, to demand respect and appreciation. It is also worth noting that the international women's movement, in its expressions and organizations, has played a role in opening up the oppressed situation of Brazilian women so they could be aware of the situation of women in different areas of the world. For example, the resistance of the *Madres de Plaza de Mayo* in Argentina, and of our sisters in Bolivia, Nicaragua, and El Salvador, has become well known and has led to solidarity and energy, which has confirmed us in the struggle, even though our contexts are different.

The persistence of women in the struggle for life and the restoration of justice have been linked together and lived out as expressions of faith, as the presence of God in the struggles of history. Many women see in these developments the expression of their desire to struggle for a more human world, in which certain values presently dormant may be aroused, where people can accept affection, where life may triumph over the powers of death.

Basic Ecclesial Communities

Finally, I want to take particular note of the work of women in basic ecclesial communities. No doubt this work has been present throughout this reflection, but I can not avoid dealing with it more fully at this point, before concluding my thoughts. I am not going to describe what women do in basic ecclesial communities. That would fill a long essay, and besides it is well known to all of us.

I would simply like to emphasize how their active role is prefiguring within the Christian churches a new way of organizing ministries. Even though these ministries are not sanctioned by church officials, they are recognized by the poorest, those to whom this service is especially directed. The new element in this service is found in the way it responds to a certain number of the community's vital needs and in the fear that it is generating in those who are in charge of the churches and who are gradually losing their former prestige. Women's ministry is shaking up men's ministry, challenging their practice and the exercise of their authority. This is taking place, not because of some decision taken by women to make it happen, but because of the nature and quality of their service and of the new social role that they are winning in the world. To the extent that women actively move onstage in the churches, their organizations, institutions, and expressions must be revised to meet the challenges continually posed by today's world.

In Conclusion: My Hope for the Future

Theological formulations that are extremely machistic, privileges of power over what is sacred, and the need for male legitimation for things to "happen" in the churches are beginning to be affected by the clashes that hint of the future. Such a statement in no way intends to replace the "masculine" model with the "feminine" one but to anticipate a new synthesis in which the dialectic present in human existence can take place, without destroying any of its vital elements.

This is my hope: The day will come when all people, lifting their eyes, will see the earth shining with brotherhood and sisterhood, mutual appreciation, true complementarity. . . .

Men and women will dwell in their houses; men and women will eat the same bread, drink the same wine, and dance together in the brightly lit square, celebrating the bonds uniting all humanity.

3

The Concept of God: A Feminine Perspective

Alida Verhoeven

We are now quite aware of the fact that the language, images and symbols which have been used to talk about God are the products of men's thinking, and that their use has been perpetuated by men. Complete philosophical, scientific, technical, and ideological systems have been set up with this language, these images, and symbols. Eventually it was passed on to the following generations through a system of teaching and learning which promoted individual success and the hierarchy of persons in a pyramid of knowledge. This system erected a few persons as masters over the life and death of the majority.

Today we say, "Enough! It's over." Never again will we use a language, an image, or a symbol that excludes the life, experience, and reflection of millions of human beings: women, young people, peoples and nations of other races or skin colors.

The Creative Task

Along with many other women we are engaged in a creative task. We want to reclaim long-term and recent memory, and to

---

Translated from the Spanish by Jeltje Aukema.

activate a creative spiritual power in the history of humankind. In order to do this, it seems necessary to go beyond the cultural-historical legacy of the Hebrew Bible and New Testament and the so-called Eastern and Western Christian traditions. Our search will include the cultural and historical legacies of people and nations with other lifestyles, forms of expression, and spiritual reflections.

The Hermeneutical Suspicion

Our hermeneutical suspicion is that the life and reflection of human beings born, raised, and trained in the Christian tradition (Eastern and Western) was almost immediately caught up in a new straitjacket after Jesus tried to free the people and tradition of Israel from the straitjacket of pharisaical law.

In Latin America, the straitjacket is an apt symbol of the horrendous and unimaginable tortures, deaths, and disappearances of which too many of our people have been victims. One by one, with the outrage of those who live, think, and act differently, the cords holding together the forced harmony of ''sound doctrine'', ''good morals'', and ''Christian ethics'' are falling off. Bit by bit the stitches holding the braces and the tacking to the very cloth of this straitjacket are coming loose.

Question: How can we think, speak, and project God for today and tomorrow? What language, image, and symbol will reflect our intimate experience of this living creative Presence? What will reflect this presence in such a way that it can continue to nourish, inspire, and strengthen those who find themselves in circumstances that are really inhumane: circumstances of suffering, oppression, injustice, and the growing threat of annihilation of life itself in our land.

Our Point of Departure: The Experiences of Women and Their Insights

The following are the testimonies of several women whose experiences are valuable for our search.

Ella is forty-one years old. She is a housewife; the mother of two children. Her husband has been missing since April 1977. Ella was born at an outpost in Mapuche territory to a girl of fourteen who did not know who the father of her child was. She was raised by her grandmother as her own daughter—with help from her aunts and uncles (among them, her mother). Ella was taught the catechism, sound doctrine, morality, ethics, and Christian values.

She says: I was taught that God controls everything, good and bad. If something bad happened to you it was because you had done something bad, you deserved to suffer, and you had to resign yourself to that. There was nothing you could do about it. If something good happened it was because you were being rewarded. So, if you were born like I was, poor and illegitimate, you would not be able to go beyond that; there was nothing you could do about it. People would look at me strangely, as though there was something wrong with me. I wasn't allowed to play with the others; nothing I did was acknowledged as worth anything.

One day I said to myself: "It shouldn't be this way." And, I decided I could do more and be more. I said: "I have the ability to do it and I have to do it." I struggled and I am still struggling to make myself better. Of course, I couldn't have done it alone. There were many who helped me and others like me. This is how I learned to accept help from others, to accept a hand outstretched in solidarity—from whatever quarter, from anyone no matter what their class or race.

This is how I found out that the teaching I had received as a girl wasn't right. Later, in those anxious times after my husband disappeared, I learned through hard knocks to fight, reflect, and unlearn what I had been taught. When they took my husband away, I saw men, flesh and blood men armed to the teeth, trained to terrorize, trample, and annihilate anyone who got in the way of the interests of the powerful. I told myself: "This evil doesn't have anything to do with God, it has to do with people. If God is like a father—like my husband is for his children—God wouldn't be so mean or cruel to his children. No, I can't believe the image of God I was taught. I'm not sure how to think of God but I know that the help I've been given has helped me feel God; I feel a Presence, a Spiritual Force around us, it moves us. I can't give it a form. It is a force that does not leave us alone. It belongs to the space where we work together, trying to ease the pain of these difficult times, listening to each other, supporting each other, and also constructively criticizing each other, always with the objective of building something better. This is what makes me feel like I'm worth something, and pushes me on."

Elsa is fifty-three years old. Although she says that she was never a communicant, she attended religious schools run by nuns from kindergarten until university.

Elsa is married, a housewife, the mother of two daughters and one son. Both of her daughters were abducted, and the son was imprisoned. One of the daughters was released, the other is still missing. Her son is in exile. Her husband is very ill; so much pain and loss has been too difficult for him to bear.

Elsa says: "In running around trying to find someone to help us, to listen to our troubles when our children were abducted, I found that even those institutions I thought were there to help could do nothing. I realized that there were many others in the same situation as we were and we had all run up against the same wall. It was worst for those of us who professed to believe in the Christian faith and believed in a just Roman Catholic Church when those doors, too, were closed on us. It was then that I understood we had been given a God and a faith packaged according to the ambitions of *men,* who had set themselves up as leaders (the clergy) of the Roman Catholic Church—totally in contrast to the Way of Jesus. This consciousness-raising, in me and many others, leads me to affirm that this predominance of the male hierarchy is ending.

I understand now that the Divinity, the divine being, is the same for all religions, Christians, Muslim, Jewish, Buddhist, and Hindu. I think that this divine being values us for how we live and not for being hypocrites. I believe that Christ is in every human being that comes to us, and as such I must value, welcome, and accept her or him so that we can work together for good and for peace."

Another woman, single, forty-seven years old with several years of pastoral experience, says: "After they abducted my boyfriend, our family tried every possible avenue; they searched for information regarding his whereabouts, tried everything in order to find out what had happened to him. We got no answers. It was always the same line. This futile search increased my suspicion that the system of beliefs, the images, phrases, and prayers that we had been taught and told to pass on to the next generation weren't true; they were empty.

"I decided to look for a new way to live, and a new expression of spirituality. I search for ways that are within my reach, that aren't based on traditional masculine methods of philosophical logic. I look for alternatives. From time to time I go back to the old ways, taking and using what I can; but for the most part, wherever possible, I try to put a wedge into the old way, to split it apart and to encourage different ways of thinking, being, and doing.''

Contributions from Other Times and Places

These stories are very similar to those of women from other places and times. Other women have discovered that the image and concept of God that has been passed down over the last thirty centuries has been conveniently ''packaged'' to accommodate the interests of those in power.

The contribution of Merlin Stone, an archeologist and sculptor, comes to mind because her artistic interest in religious objects has led her from one astonishing find to another in her excavations in the Middle East. In digging from one layer to the next, she has found goddess figures. Objects like these help the archeologists give us a better understanding of what life was like in those times. According to the evidence, life then was more harmonious; there was more real ecumenical sharing of resources among men and women.

Merlin Stone denounces the invasion of a culture based on the physical and mental forcefulness of men that destroyed the vestiges of women's values, feelings, expressions, and spiritual life. Wherever these different ways of thinking and living appeared, the people were persecuted terribly, their places of worship were burned, and there were witch hunts. Then, the masculine god was imposed upon them with all that entailed, including masculine ways of thinking and acting. Stone notes that it was here in the ''cradle'' of the Middle East that the three great spiritual currents of our history were born and developed. All reflect predominately male ways of thinking, speech, and symbols. In each of these, women are inevitably given servant roles, particularly in the religious ceremonies in temples or holy places.

Stories of the different projects begun by women in order to recreate values, language, images, and spiritual symbols fill several library shelves. In 1895, Elizabeth Cady Stanton wrote the *Women's Bible*. Nevertheless, I suspect that in spite of these contributions there is still a vacuum regarding appropriate language, images, and symbols. Even though we don't want to be, we ourselves are trapped in the same game of intellectual excellence. So we are invited to contribute, to increase the number of articles and books on theology—in this case, liberation theology. This effort does not really liberate us; in fact, by encouraging us to do (male) scientific work, we fall into the same trap. We see ourselves succeeding as solitary women who have achieved recognition in a man's world. By doing this we simply perpetuate the present situation.

Our Vocation

Perhaps we are called to close a "fraudulent era" and fill this vacuum of language, image, and symbol with a consciousness (collective wisdom) of the Creative Spiritual Force that can no longer be trapped by language, images, or symbols. This Force manifests itself only in vital-creative-presence for life. It is both being and becoming in everything that promotes life, love, justice, and peace.

If this is our vocation we face the beginning of an exodus. An exodus from all the limitations that have been imposed on us, and from all the niceties to which we have become accustomed. We will begin the difficult crossing of this space (wilderness) on the margin of culture and the religious expression we have rejected; yet it is here that we must carve out spaces in order to recreate a culture. It will involve a difficult crossing of our own interiors as well, so that we can see, feel, and affirm who we are, making room for self-criticism. Crossing this unknown territory means we run the risk of losing our way, but here every bit of acknowledgment, approval, and mutual understanding is like water pouring out of a rock and manna from heaven. Finally, we will come to a place where no one lives off of another, but where the lives of all are valued and they live together in justice, peace, and love.

Conclusion

The theme that was announced for our meeting of women theologians is contradictory to our feminine perception. We can no longer include an essay on the "Concept of God" in a theology done from women's perspective. From our perspective the Presence of Creative-Recreative Spiritual Force, the source of Life and Love, is like an ongoing movement, an ebb and flow that moves in growing waves that wash over everything. It is like throwing a rock into a still pond; the ripples spread out wider and wider until they reach the shore where they seem to bounce back toward the spot from which they started; it affects the whole surface of the pond. Nothing and no one is unaffected by the movement of this creative and recreative spiritual force. The future is wide open to its movement; and it is this movement that is the guarantee for the Life that seems so threatened today. It is also this movement that assures us that the spiritual and psychic perceptions that infuse our women-being are valid for the process of re-creation to which we are called. We women have a special ability to understand the heart of nature and to feel the pulse of the cosmos for the creative fullness that is produced in our very beings. We need only take time to stop and listen to the spiritual voice deep inside ourselves in order to begin the transformation, and from there to extend it in growing circles until it reaches all women, communities, the world, and the entire universe.

4

Reflections on the Trinity

María Clara Bingemer

Our primary objective is to trace the clues leading to the revelation of the feminine in God. By the end of our search, we should be able to believe in and call on God using feminine appellation without having strayed from the Church or the Good News of Jesus Christ. We know that our study is not the first on this subject. Over the last few years, even more over the last few decades, many valuable articles have been written on this theme.[1] This does not mean, however, that there is nothing more to be said. On the contrary. While still part of a larger context of the poor and all marginalized peoples' struggle for liberation, the problems facing women in Latin America have particular twists and specific considerations. We believe that there is a special need in Latin America for careful reflection on the theme of the Trinity from woman's perspective.

Any search for theological expression geared toward finding new ways must be centered on the main mystery, the source, on the basis of the Christian faith and theology: God. There is a legitimate theological basis for women's struggle to be partners with men, working with them, side by side rather than as inferior or lesser beings. We can say this because we believe that the divine being that created, saves, and sanctifies us does not identify with one

---

Translated from the Spanish by Jeltje Aukema.

gender more than the other. On the contrary, while God transcends them, God brings men and women together without suppressing the richness of their differences.

We believe that there is a feminine as well as masculine principle in our creation in the image of God, in our salvation made possible by the Incarnation, Passion, and Resurrection of Jesus Christ, and in our new being shaped by God's Spirit. Nevertheless, the masculine principle has been made much more widely recognized. It is all the more important, then, that this feminine principle be taken out of hiding, out of the corner in which it has been kept over all these years of Judeo-Christian patriarchalism. It is time for it to rise to the fore and take its proper place. A faith in God that is identified only with masculine traits is incompatible with Christian revelation and with the God of love.

We hope to uncover some of the hidden feminine aspects of the revelation of the trinitarian mystery of God. These aspects will add to, and enrich, our reflection while at the same time give our beliefs solid foundation. Having done this we will draw several conclusions which, even though they must remain open ended and provisional, can perhaps contribute to growth in our lives as Christians and to our theological reflection on women today in Latin America. These conclusions are related to anthropology and social relationships, and to the global struggle for liberation from any kind of oppression.

However, it is first necessary to examine briefly our situation so that we will know why we face the problems we do today. Why are the language and images used by the Christian faith to convey the central mystery of our beliefs so markedly masculine? For example, Father, Lord, Omnipotent, Warrior, Son. What are the cultural, anthropological, and theological problems encountered in the roots of this kind of language and typology?

The Beginnings of the Problem: A Triple Dualism

We will start with *anthropological theology* because it tells us that the human being is the image of God. Now, in examining the concept that we have of the image (human being), analogically we see the characteristics of our model (God). In the Judeo-Christian world, and still today in so-called Western Christian civilization, this concept is decidedly *androcentric*. Even if one puts the two literary traditions of the creation story, Yahwist (Genesis 2:18–24) and Priestly (Genesis 1:26–27), which was written later, together to form one story, it still comes out hierarchical. Woman is created *after* and *from* man. This makes for the ontological, biological, and sociological dependence of women on men. What has even more serious implications for our study is the idea that only the male gender is *theomorphous* (has the form and image of God). This typology, as it affects all subsequent theological work, makes for what may be called "theological sexology."[2] Throughout biblical tradition in the economy of the covenant, that which is divine (God, Jesus Christ) is represented with masculine elements and that which is human (Israel, the Church) with feminine elements. Androcentrism and theocentrism are parallel.

In later doctrine, most notably in the work of Saint Augustine which indelibly marked the West, woman can be considered the image of God in her rational soul, but not in her feminine sexual body, in which form she is, in fact, subordinate to men. On the other hand, the male gender in itself symbolizes the excellence of the divine image. With this kind of body-soul dualism, man is *theomorphous* in the primary sense. And God, the universal God of all peoples for all times becomes *andromorphous*. It is not difficult to see why God is always called king, judge, patriarch, husband, lord, and father. Along with this notion of male supremacy in traditional theology is the idea that woman can only reach this coveted level when she loses her femininity, that is, when she renounces the functions proper to her gender, and by so doing transcends her auxiliary function of procreation.[3] The damaging extent and consequences of the body-soul dualism that determines this anthropology are revealed when it is applied to God's image. There is a gap between humanity and femininity. As long as she is female, a woman is not the image of God; thus, in order to be saved (that is, in order to become one with God) she must find another form. Women must stop being women and take on masculine characteristics. The "bottom line," as it were, is that while women have no direct access, no place, no identity, and do not belong to the intimate mysteries of God, men, by the very fact that they are men, have direct access and position. A god that goes along with this is a god who gives privileges to and identifies with only one gender.[4]

The *second dualism* is associated with the beginnings of the idea that God is predominately masculine; it refers to worldview. This worldview makes a static separation between the *earth* and the *heavens,* between that which is above, invisible, and transcendent and that which is below, palpable, and immanent. We have learned from history; today, through modern discoveries in religious psychology we know that the divinity or divine being, as it appears in all cultures in all times, always represents cultural archetypal symbolism, be it paternal or maternal. With this archetypal symbolism we are referred to two basic religious types:

> . . . The one type is chthonic or telluric—oriented toward earth, life, generation, and the mysteries of death. This is the maternal religion. The other is uranic or celestial, and is oriented toward the sky, infinity, and transcendence. This is the paternal religion. The former concentrates more on our origin, and original earthly paradise, and the primordial state of our reconciliation. The latter is turned rather toward the end of history, and seeks salvation and a future Reign of God. The one accents generation and conception; the other, birth.[5]

In this way, Judaism and Christianity are now and always have been eminently uranic, or masculine religions. In the case of Judaism, its characteristic monotheism was formed on the basis of Israel's rupture with the religions of its neighbors, who identified their feminine divinities with nature and its cycles: the earth, fertility, the moon, etc. The uranic or masculine aspects of Christianity were affirmed with the incarnation of God in the man Jesus and in the promise of a Kingdom for the future. Over the centuries, with a predominant emphasis on the vertical and an anthropology which portrays God as masculine, the religious practices related to Christianity and Judaism gave the heavens more importance than the earth. (In contrast to telluric religions which emphasized the horizontal and focused on the mysteries of life and death.) This emphasis on the heavenly over the earthly, the vertical over the horizontal, and the future over against the beginning, greatly affected how they saw the being and essence of God. It is clearer now that there is little relationship between this God and Jesus' *Abba*. "On the contrary, this patriarchal God was born with the first division of the world into heaven and earth. . . ."[6]

A *third dualism* follows directly from the other two. It has to do with that which shapes modern society: the dualism between efficiency and gratuity, pragmatism and experience, action and contemplation. Modern society is particularly active and it places a high value on action that brings change, inventive abilities, organization, productivity, and control. In short, the attributes that are understood as, and identified with, being masculine. On the other end of the human spectrum are those attributes usually identified as feminine: receptivity, passivity, grace, the care and protection of life, intuitive perception and choice. These attributes are often minimized; they are considered useless or lesser for not being effective or productive. It is not surprising that the qualities attributed to a society's god are the qualities valued within that society. The God of modern society is strong, powerful, absolutely transcendent, Lord, Dominator. The strength of this God brought the Hebrews out of slavery in Egypt. Service to this Lord means having carefully laid plans and feverish activity, characterized by efficiency and a sense of urgency. This emphasis on power and dominion means that the characteristics of the dominated,[7] such as weakness, subjection, and inferiority are looked down upon, along with anything that looks like passivity, receptivity, or gratuity. The image of the patriarchal God that marks Judaism and Christianity, particularly during certain periods of its history, is closely linked to men's position of power in society. These links are most obvious in the emphasis on the transcendent at the expense of the immanent, of life on earth, and of the living out of love and friendship.

Our objective is to try to show that the dualisms described above, and the consequences of these dualisms, find no absolute foundation in Christian revelation. Although we find predominantly masculine aspects in the Scriptures and in theology—and we have to admit, they certainly are there—we can also find some feminine and motherly traits in God. These traits are few and scattered. Yet, the fact that we find any at all is most amazing. These few obvious examples have penetrated the monolithic patriarchal blockade like the tip of an iceberg with points to an immense underworld to be discovered. If this much appears on the surface, imagine what we might find in the depths!

The feminine language and images that peek through the Scriptures let us see God's feminine traits. Thus, we can call on God not only as a strong Father but also like a Mother who is supportive, consoling, and protective; and also as the Spirit of creativity, balance, and beauty. The God of Christianity is not a lone patriarch and dominator who is permanently located far away in the heavens. Rather, this God is a community of love between persons (Father, Son, Holy Spirit) where the differences and pluralities are not suppressed but integrated; where masculine force is enriched and complemented by feminine tenderness; where life is a whole process of begetting and being born. In this divine community, the human community finds its likeness. The poor and the marginalized are included as responsible subjects of history. Among these, women find themselves, face to face, partners with men in human dignity; women, like men, are the image of God.

Possible Openings for a Feminist Trinitarian Theology

Having addressed the cultural and theological problems associated with the masculine concept of God in Western Christianity, we are now prepared to propose perspectives which might lead to a new reading. What is there to indicate that feminine, as well as masculine, aspects are not simply a product of our imagination but really have roots in Christian revelation? On what can we base our argument that the God we believe in and whom we worship as Father, Son, and Holy Spirit has a truly feminine dimension? In order to do this we will first support our argument with what has already been revealed about God in the Bible and in the history of the Church.

Feminine Characteristics of the God of the Bible

We will begin by looking at a few of the terms used in the Hebrew Bible and New Testament to refer to God and which afford access to the feminine reality of God's mystery. Then, we will study a few of the images that communicate the divine mystery.

One of the biblical terms often used in referring to God is *rachamim*. It describes God's mercy. The root of the word is *rechem* which means mother's breast, or womb;[8] *rachamim* then, refers to that safe place in a woman's body where a child is conceived, nourished, protected, where it grows and later is given birth.

Rachamim is used to compare God's love to that of a mother.

Pope John Paul II mentions *rachamim* in the Encyclical *Dives in Misericordia:*

> From the deep and original bond—indeed the unity—that links a mother to her child there springs a particular relationship to the child, a particular love. Of this love one can say that it is completely gratuitous, not merited, and that in this aspect it constitutes an interior necessity: an exigency of the heart. It is, as it were, a "feminine" variation of the masculine fidelity to self expressed by *chesed.* Against this psychological background, *rachamim* generates a whole range of feelings, including goodness and tenderness, patience and understanding, that is, readiness to forgive.[9]

In Isaiah 49:15, God is compared with a mother.

> Does a woman forget her baby at the breast,
> or fail to cherish the son of her womb?
> Yet even if these forget,
> I will never forget you.

Jeremiah 31:20 refers to God's *rachamim.*

> Is Ephraim my dear son?
> Is he my darling child?
> For as often as I speak against him,
> I do remember him still.
> Therefore my heart [womb] yearns for him;
> I will surely have mercy on him, says the Lord.
> (RSV)

Isaiah 42:14 suggests that the sufferings of God for God's children are like the pains of childbirth.

> "From the beginning I have been silent,
> I have kept quiet, held myself in check.
> I groan like a woman in labor,
> I suffocate, I stifle."

This faithful, invincible love, thanks to the mysterious intimacy of motherhood, is expressed in many different ways in the Hebrew Bible. It is expressed as protection and salvation from dangers and different enemies, as pardon for the sins of the people, and also as faithfulness in keeping promises and in boosting hope, in spite of the infidelity of others (Hos. 14:5; Isa. 45:8–10; 55:7; Mic. 7:19; Dan. 9:9). The *chesed* of God, God's profound mercy, God's faithfulness to the people in spite of their infidelity and sin, comes from God's motherly heart, *rachamim;* God will always be compassionate and infinitely tender (Isaiah 14:1).

The faith of Israel is directed toward this God as toward its mother's womb. It calls and asks for loving protection.

> Where is your ardor, your might,
> the yearning of your inmost heart?
> Do not let your compassion go unmoved . . .
> (Isaiah 63:15)

> Has God forgotten to show mercy,
> or has his anger overcome his tenderness?
> (Psalm 77:9)[10]

Psalm 79:8 calls for the divine *rachamim* as for God.

> Do not hold our ancestors' crimes against us,
> in tenderness quickly intervene,
> we can hardly be crushed lower;
> help us, God our savior . . .[11]

Why can't the same God who is known and adored by the chosen people as a strong liberator, a dread warrior, and a powerful Lord also be known as a loving and tender mother?

The term *ruach* is also helpful. In the Hebrew Bible it means "wind," "spirit" or "breath of life;" it is feminine in gender. Sometimes in the Hebrew Bible this wind is a soft breeze, other times it is a forceful gale (I Kings 19:11; Isa. 57:13 and others). At times God sends the wind (Ezek. 1:4; Dan. 7:2), other times God is in the wind, it is God's breath, life (2 Sam. 22:16; Ps. 18:16;

Isa. 11:15, etc.). *Ruach* is the presence of God, the bearer and cause of life.

Keeping our theme in mind, we want to call special attention to the signs of the divine *ruach.* It is mentioned in the creation of the world (Gen. 1:2) when the *ruach* moved over the earth.[12] Paul Evdokimov, a great Russian orthodox theologian, says this about woman: "She is under the sign of the Spirit which, in the creation narrative, covers the egg of the earth."[13] The Spirit appears as a Great Mother who gives birth to the world from her generous and loving womb. This same *ruach,* the mother of life, gives the breath of life (Ezek. 36, 37; 1 Sam. 10:6–10; 2 Kings 3:15ff). In other passages *ruach* appears as God (Isa. 63:10–11; Ps. 51:13), which is later a basis for the Holy Spirit (Mark 1:9–11 and parallels). In Syriac texts this Spirit is called the Consoler (feminine).[14]

There are other significant terms in the Hebrew Bible, for example, Wisdom *(hochmah, sophia),* described as being the daughter of God. With her, God creates. Solomon calls Wisdom the "wife of my soul" (Wisd. 7–10). In Proverbs 8:23–31, the same Wisdom that is the mediator of creation, is imagined as a mother who passes on wisdom to her children. The author of the book of Wisdom portrays wisdom as a feminine presence, God's mediator, throughout the whole of the history of salvation of God's chosen people. She was their companion and guide; she helped them in trouble and danger. Once she passed with them through the Red Sea; she "opened the mouths of the dumb and gave speech to the tongues of babes" (Wisd. 10:21) so that they could give praise to Yahweh. The theology of Wisdom has to do with divine nature as it is known and acted out in the lives of human beings. It is God in as much as it is the force of creation, never dissolved or diluted; it receives its real being from God; it lives from and is rewarded by God.

> What is described is a "feminine" type of presence and activity. It is useful to compare the account of creation in the first few chapters of Genesis, with the description of the activity of Wisdom in creation (Wisdom 7–8). In the former, God forms and "places" created things. We watch him making the world. He views it *from without,* and is satisfied. This is a masculine image of conscious, visible, reasonable planning. In the Wisdom passages we see "creation from within"

> a continuous process of "ordering," shaping, inspiring, sustaining, changing. It is equally the work of "omnipotence," but it works *within* the situation, and can only be properly grasped by one who, himself, "lives with Wisdom."[15]

The image of *Sophia* disappears in rabbinic literature with the advent of the Christian era, perhaps because of its use in gnosticism. Nevertheless, it reappears in the form of *Shekinah,* a new feminine mediator image of God in the midst of the people. *Shekinah* is responsible for the reconciliation of Israel with God; and, in the rabbis' mystic speculation about the exile, *Shekinah* is imagined as going into exile with Israel when God's face was hidden from the people.

> Each Shabbat celebration is seen as a mystical connubial embrace of God with his *Shekinah,* anticipating the final reunion of God with creation in the messianic age. The exile of Israel from the land is seen ultimately as an exile within God, divorcing the masculine from the feminine "side" of God.[16]

More recently, in Orthodox thought, Sergius Bulgakov[17] relates sophiology (that which is related to the Wisdom of God) with the *ousia* or Being of God. Sophia, then, would be the matrix or the foundation of being of the three divine persons.

In the New Testament we do not find the same kinds of feminine images applied to God as we found in the Hebrew Bible. Jesus, the Son of God, is obviously a man. He refers to God as Abba-Father, definitely a masculine appellative. The Holy Spirit, the third person of the Trinity is called *Pneuma* in Greek. The gender of this word is neutral, neither masculine nor feminine. There is, however, a word used in the Johannine writings that has strong roots in Christian tradition and refers to the mystery of God. The word is *agape* which we translate as "love." "God is love" (I John 4:8–16). We believe that this word is helpful, not because it has a feminine gender in Greek, but for the profound reality that it expresses. John's *agape* is the love of God that comes from above and flows over the world, encouraging loving relationships and communion which eventually return to God.

> . . . In brotherly love the circle of the Father, the Son, and the people of the Son constitutes a fellowship which is not of this world. The love of God is the final reality for the life of this fellowship, and abiding in his love is the law of life.[18]

God's love for humankind, as it flows out of the trinitarian economy, is the image and form of God's deepest reality. The love of this mysterious reality is inclusive; the poor and the "lesser" people have high positions; women and men live in harmony. The semantics which label God as agape, "love," provide the perfect setting for the eucharistic banquet[19] where again we can see feminine aspects of the Trinity.[20] Let's go back to the Bible now to look beyond these semantic clues for feminine images of God.

The first image we come across is found in the Priestly account of creation in Genesis. Here the human being, both man and woman, appears as the true image of God: "Let us make man in our own image, in the likeness of ourselves . . ." (Gen. 1:26). In this passage, the plural is used in referring to God. Some of the Church Fathers declared this to be a "hint" of the Trinity.[21] *Man* is used in the collective sense, as in *humankind.* The plural is used again later on in the text: ". . . let them be masters of the fish of the sea, the birds of heaven. . . . God created man in the image of himself, in the image of God he created him, male and female he created them" (vs. 26,27).

In this context, the difference between man and woman does not seem to be a hierarchical difference. There seems to be a reciprocity in their relationship that reflects the relationship between the divine persons. Thus, in the intimacy of the Spirit, the Father is simply a Father to his Son and vice versa. So too, man is simply a man to woman and vice versa, as in the trinitarian analogy.

> . . . This reciprocity is the first and last element. Just as the Son and the Holy Spirit constitute references to an unprincipiated Principle, an absolute Mystery, the Father, so also man and woman are constituted by reference to a dynamism that transcends them and constitutes the mystery of the human being.[22]

There are other passages in which God is described as doing things a woman or mother would do. For example, there is the beautiful chapter in Hosea where God is teaching Ephraim to walk: "I was like someone who lifts an infant close against his cheek; stooping down to him I gave him his food" (Hosea 11:4). In Isaiah God is presented as a woman who consoles Israel (66:13); she cannot forget the child of her womb (49). The wisdom literature shows a close correlation between Woman, Wisdom, and God (Prov. 8:22–26; 19:14; 40:12; 31:10; 26:30; Sirach 24:9; Wisd. 3:12; 7:28).

In the New Testament, Jesus pictures the love of God for the sinner like a woman who has lost one of the ten coins (drachmas) she had. She lights a lamp, sweeps the house, and looks for the coin until she finds it. Then she calls her friends together to celebrate having found it (Luke 15:8–10). In another passage, Jesus cries over Jerusalem for having killed the prophets and stoned those sent to the city. He says: "How often I have longed to gather your children, as a hen gathers her brood under her wings . . . (Luke 13:34). In Revelation, the last book of the Bible, God is portrayed as making a typically motherly gesture:

> He will wipe away all tears from their eyes;
> there will be no more death,
> and no more mourning or sadness.
> The world of the past has gone (21:4).

Doesn't this scene seem like an analogy of a mother waking with a child who has had a nightmare? She wipes his eyes and comforts him until he is no longer afraid and once again feels that everything is all right and becomes quiet and sleepy.

These images provide a glimpse of the feminine aspects of the mystery of the God who is love. They allow us to affirm that there exists a feminine principle in the divinity which makes it possible to believe, worship, and love God not only as the strong Father who creates us and liberates us with his powerful arm, but also as a Mother, full of tenderness, grace, beauty, and receptivity, who accepts the seed of life and feeds it in her womb, so it may become a full being in the light of day. The breath of the Spirit that blows where it will, stirred up, in the history of the Church and in the

Christian tradition, experiences of persons who knew the feminine aspects of God in one or another of the three persons of the Trinity. With the above as our basis we will go on with our study.

Some Examples from Christian Traditions and the History of the Church

The Bible is not the only place where we are presented with examples of God's feminine traits; we also find them in the Christian tradition and Church history. We will examine a few examples which throughout the ages indicate divine revelation of God's feminine aspects. There are so many that we will have to limit ourselves to three.

The first text is a saying from the apocryphal Epistle to the Hebrews. Jesus says: "And then, my mother, the Holy Spirit, grabbed me by the hair and pointed me toward the great mountain called Tabor."[23]

The author of this apocryphal book is expressing a personal or communal experience of God as a divine mother who guides her son in the way he should go, demonstrating that such maternal images of God may be found even in the earliest Christian tradition.

Our second example is taken from the writings of Clement of Alexandria, who wrote in Egypt in around 180 A.D.:

> The word is everything to the child, both Father and Mother: teacher and nurse. The nutriment is the milk of the Father and the Word alone supplies us children with the milk of love, and only those who suck at this breast are truly happy. For this reason, seeking is called sucking; to those infants who seek the Word, the Father's loving breasts supply milk.

And, in describing divine nature, he insists:

> . . . men and women share equally in perfection, and are to receive the same instruction and the same discipline. For the name "humanity" is common to both men and women; and for us "in Christ there is neither male nor female."[24]

Much later, we have Julian of Norwich. She was an English mystic who lived during the middle of the fourteenth century as a hermit. A rare exception in her time, she received the best education available and went as far as one could go in the medieval educational system. She excelled in Latin grammar, rhetoric, and logic. At the end of her life she learned and taught theology, the highpoint of the Scholastic.[25] Her mystical experiences occurred in three distinct ways: through bodily mediated visions, spiritual visions, and the silent words that formed in her mind. Her vision of God had a masculine and a feminine face.

> And so I saw that God was happy to be our Father, and God was happy to be our Mother, and God was happy to be our true husband and that our soul would be his beloved wife.[26]

Julian's vision of the divine Mother is characteristic of her work. Having declared that motherhood is part of God's nature, she goes on to say that Jesus, in doing the work of the Father, took our soul into himself and became its mother.

> . . . our saviour is our true Mother in whom we are endlessly born and out of whom—we shall come.[27] . . . all the lovely works, all the sweet and loving offices of beloved motherhood are appropriated to the second person for in him we have this godly will, whole and safe forever, both in nature and in grace, from his own goodness proper to him.[28]

To Julian's way of thinking, we are forever carried inside of Christ. His passion and death are his pains of childbirth through which we are liberated for blessing. Yet, Christ continues working in us; he needs to feed us and he does so with his own body, sacramentally and in the teachings of the Church.[29] Julian carefully and respectfully applies this view of Christ as mother, nourishing her child with her body, to the mystery of the Eucharist. In spite of her very original mystical experiences, Julian never had major problems with the Church. On the other hand, it did not give her much recognition either. While she helped the many who came to visit her in their spiritual lives, she died in an anonymous life of prayer. Fortunately, her story was not lost; it comes to us by way of a book of her own writings as well as what others wrote about her.

In the examples above, we have seen how masculine and feminine traits can be and have been applied to each of the three persons of the Trinity.

From the Bible, we examined the words *rachamim, ruach,* and *wisdom.* We saw how God's *rachamim* was the other side of God's love, which is both paternal and maternal. The divine *ruach* is applied to the Spirit which is active in creation and in moving all things. *Wisdom* is the creative mediation of God which, in Christianity, is assumed by the *Logos,* a word quickly identified with the Son. In each of these biblical terms, there are three semantic nuclei which reveal the feminine traits of the divine which can be applied to each one of the three persons of the Trinity. The mystery of their love is described by *agape,* love which comes from above and promotes loving human relationships.

Three examples from history gave us much the same perspective: the feminine traits of God are alternately applicable to all three persons of the Trinity. The apocryphal Gospel to the Hebrews applied feminine traits to the Holy Spirit; Clement of Alexandria applied them to the Father and the Son; and Julian of Norwich applied them to the Son Incarnate, to Jesus Christ. Each person of the Trinity shows a harmonization of masculine and feminine traits. They are a community of love which has revealed itself in feminine and masculine terms. From here we can go on to the next part of our reflection.

The Feminine and the Divine Persons

We will now fix our attention on each of the three divine persons, examining in turn their feminine traits. In doing so we will dwell on what we can perceive of the mystery of divine love by means of God's salvific action among us. Contemplating this Revelation, provided by the Incarnate Son and the Spirit operating in the womb of history, permits us to arrive at the Origin without origin, where we are invited into the ineffable mystery of God's inner life. In this search for the feminine face of God, we should remember Karl Rahner's axiom: the Economic Trinity (the role of three persons in the economy of salvation) and the Immanent Trinity (the relation of the three persons within God's own being) are one. The communion of agapic love, the most intimate aspect of God, draws us. These feminine features, discerned at the level of God's intervention in history, direct us to the feminine aspects of God in the innermost part of the Mystery before which we bow down and worship.

We will begin with the second person of the Trinity, the Son incarnate, who through his incarnation, life, passion, and resurrection, opened a new, living way for us.

The Son: Founder of a Community of Men and Women

From the Gospel accounts we gather that the *historical Jesus* initiated an itinerant charismatic movement where men and women worked together as partners. It was different from the movement begun by John the Baptist which emphasized asceticism and penitence, and from the Qumran movement which admitted only men. In addition to preaching about the Kingdom, Jesus' movement was characterized by joy, a lack of prejudice (all kinds of sinners and marginalized people were welcome at meals and celebrations), and its disregard for many of the societal taboos of that time. His disregard for the taboo concerning women was one of the more significant; women in the Judaism of his time were considered socially and religiously inferior.

> . . . First, they were not circumcised and hence could not be part of God's covenant. Next, they were subject to rigorous rules of "purification," by reason of their female biological condition. Finally, they had been personified in Eve, with all the inferiority that that implied.[30]

So it was that the rabbis of that time were known for thanking God for three things: for not having been born a Gentile, not being ignorant of the law, and for not having been born a woman. In this context, Jesus' practices were not only innovative, but shocking. None of Jesus' teachings directly addressed this issue, but his attitude toward women was considered unusual for this time, even by his disciples (John 4:27).

The idea that women are part of the Kingdom and that they are called by Jesus, not only as contributors but as active participants (Luke 10:38–42) as well as privileged beneficiaries of his miracles, is found in all four Gospels (Luke 8:2; Mark 1:29–31; 5:25–34; 7:24–30 and others).

Jesus' attitude toward women has theological significance for us today. First of all it points toward the most important aspect of the Gospel: the Good News announced to the poor. Jesus wanted to free those who were disinherited, rejected, sinners, pagans, marginalized in any way, including women and children who were not considered very important by Jewish society. Jesus gave these people privileged places in his Kingdom; he integrated them into the community of the children of God. With the guidance of God the Father and the Holy Spirit, he was able to discern in the poor (among them women) value that others overlooked: "the precious life of the trampled reed or the fire on the wick that smokes but will not go out."[31]

Jesus' liberating praxis in regard to women tore down and destroyed one of the three dualisms we mentioned earlier: the body-soul dualism. By accepting women as they were, including their bodies, considered weak and unclean in their own culture, Jesus announced an integrated anthropology that valued the human being, composed of body and soul. The following are instances recorded in the Gospels where Jesus did not shun bodily contact with women.

- He allowed a woman who had been hemorrhaging for twelve years to touch his cloak, thereby risking impurity, according to Jewish law (Matt. 9:20–22).
- He revived Jairus' dead daughter by taking her hand (Matt. 9:18–29).
- He allowed a known sinner to touch him, kiss him, and anoint his feet, thus, for his host, casting doubt on his prophetic answer (Luke 7:36–50).

The dualism we referred to above was a later development in Christian thought; it certainly did not have its roots in Jesus' teaching and practice.

Having addressed Jesus' attitudes toward women, we will now turn to that which is *feminine in Jesus*. There is an opening for this kind of inquiry in modern psychology, which tells us that every human being is at the same time and in different proportions both *animus* and *anima,* masculine and feminine.[32] If this idea which is so widely accepted today is true, then Jesus, who was predominately masculine, also had a feminine dimension. Jesus, overcoming the androcentrism of his time,

> . . . integrated within himself so many behavioral characteristics, both feminine and masculine, that we can consider him to be the first fully mature person.[33]

The gospels portray Jesus as a man who was not ashamed of his own feelings. Thus, he was able to speak harshly and reproach the Pharisees and disciples, singing joyful and grateful praise to God for revealing God's revelation to mere children while hiding it from the learned and clever (Matt. 11:25–27). We dare say that in the depth of his being, Jesus felt the emotion and the pain that afflicted the *rachamim* of Yahweh in the Hebrew Bible. We see this emotion in Jesus when he cries for his dead friend Lazarus (John 11:35), mourns over the city that will be held responsible for his martyrdom (Luke 19:41), laments the misfortune of the cities that refused to repent (Matt. 11:21), and in his admonishment of the ''little chicks'' of Jerusalem whom he wished to take under his wings (Luke 13:34).

All these feminine aspects of Jesus—his tenderness, compassion, and infinite mercy—were fully realized in his sorrowful birth on the cross.[34] These qualities were assumed, eternally, definitively, and hypostatically, by the Word, the second person of the Trinity. Thus, we can say that in Jesus, in his life, words, praxis, and his person—in all that is most intimate to his being—that which is feminine is divinized and belongs to the most profound mystery of the love of God.[35]

The Spirit: Uncreated Motherly Love

Faith and the Scriptures tell us that in Jesus' absence the Spirit takes his place in the community of faith, like ''another Paraclete'' who lives among us, on the side of the baptized as their defense and comfort.

According to the Gospel of John, several of Jesus' references to the Spirit have motherly connotations. The Spirit will not abandon us as orphans (John 14:18); the Spirit consoles, exhorts, and comforts us as loving mother (14:26). Paul talks about the Spirit as doing things usually done by a mother: teaching us to stammer the names of the Abba-Father (Romans 8:15) and Jesus Christ (1 Cor. 12:3); teaching us how to pray in a way that is acceptable and pleasing to God (Rom. 8:26).[36] The Hebrew term *ruach,*[37] ancestor of the New Testament word *pneuma,* in addition to being feminine in gender is often linked to creation, the beginnings of and the protection of life: functions usually associated with motherhood.

In ancient Christianity, the apocryphal Gospel to the Hebrews,[38] cited above, was referred to by Origen in his commentary on John and by St. Jerome: they both used it to talk about the divine maternalism of the Holy Spirit.

One of the first Syriac Fathers, Aphrahat, called the "Wise One of Persia" (345 A.D.), wrote the following in his "Sermon About Virginity":

> We learn from the Law: ". . . man leaves his father and mother and joins himself to his wife, and they become one body" (Genesis 2:24). This is a great and noble prophecy. But, who then is father and mother to the man who leaves his own to take a wife? This means that in taking a wife, a man loves and honors God his Father and the Holy Spirit his Mother; and he will have no other love.[39]

Makarios, a Syriac Father adds:

> The Spirit is our Mother because the Paraclete or Comforter is ready to console us like a mother consoles her child (Isa. 66:13) and because believers, "reborn" in the Spirit, are children of the mysterious mother, the Holy Spirit (John 3:3–5).[40]

Can theology seriously support this idea of the motherhood of the Holy Spirit? There are many theologians leaning in this direction.[41] However, in this essay we will follow a more prudent line and affirm, with the Council of Ephesius (431 A.D.), that the mother of Jesus is Mary, the *Theotokos.* Nevertheless, along with our affirmation of this statement, which attributes Mary's conception of Jesus to the Holy Spirit, we can also affirm that the Holy Spirit is Uncreated Love, which proceeded from the Father to make Mary pregnant. It is difficult to separate the Father from the Spirit as Father and Mother of the incarnate Son; only because God is one in three persons can we say that the Spirit is a distinct person from the Father, with its own functions and works. Yet, if we can say that the conception of the Word in Mary is a work of the Father, we can at the same time affirm that this work of the Father is realized through the Holy Spirit, Maternal Love. If it is a delicate matter to affirm that the Holy Spirit is the "Divine Mother" of the man Jesus of Nazareth, one can say without the shadow of a doubt that the Holy Spirit, the *ruach* of the Hebrew Bible and the *pneuma* of the New Testament,

> . . . is the divine-maternal Love in the Father in relationship to the divinely conceived Christ; it is the same divine-maternal Love in the Virgin in relationship to the humanly conceived Christ.[42]

The divine-maternal Love that is fleshed out in Mary lets Christians imagine, through her, the maternal face of God,[43] and through her, the Holy Spirit gives us an understanding of the image of God that would not be possible in any other way. This discovery of the feminine and maternal dimension of the Holy Spirit breaks the body-soul, earth-heaven dualisms that we have said were the beginnings of the predominance of the masculine God, and it provides us with the opportunity to appreciate the whole human being. The indwelling of the Holy Spirit in human beings, body and soul, enables them to be ready and open receptacles for the grace of God. The presence of the Holy Spirit flows out over the whole world ordering chaos and transforming all of creation, even the most insignificant of earthly things, so that they can sing God's praises.

This view of the Holy Spirit with its feminine and maternal characteristics makes it possible for us to feel that we "are not only *under God* but *in God.*"[44] This frees us from false images of a monotheistic God and helps us experience the fullness of God, with our whole being, within the community of men and women where the helpless and exploited ones of this world, the orphans, widows, the poor and the alien have a secure place in our midst, are cared for, loved, and protected.

The Maternal Father and the Paternal Mother

The Son and the Holy Spirit lead us to the invisible Father, the Abba of eternal love, the Beginning without beginning, Mystery without end. This Mystery is the most excellent expression of all fatherhood—called by Jesus *Abba-Father!* Whether in joy (Matt. 11:25–27), in distress (Mark 14:32–42), or in solemn devotion (John 17:1f). Can theology find in this Father any feminine or maternal traits? Would the Father of Jesus, the great mystery of the Christian faith allow in himself, in his person, maternal aspects?

We will begin our reflection on the Father with this quote from the Gospels:

> . . . no one knows the Son except the Father, just as no one knows the Father except the Son and those to whom the Son chooses to reveal him (Matt. 11:27).

Above all then, God the Father is the Father of Jesus Christ. Only Jesus' relationship with the Father can be the key to the interpretation of God's paternity. And, the only possible way to enter into the mystery of this relationship is through the inspiration of the Holy Spirit. Any attempt to understand the maternal aspects of the Father must go through the Trinity.

The Father whom many believers claim to worship as Christ is really solitary, invulnerable, and impassible. This idea is far from the biblical idea of God. As we have already seen in our study, the God of the Bible who is the powerful Lord, dread Warrior, Creator of all that is, is at the same time a God of mercy and tenderness, whose mercy *(chesed)* endures from generation to generation. This God's depths of mercy are likened to a womb *(rachamim)* that is moved in compassion for the beloved son.

This God of the womb is none other than the Father of our Lord Jesus Christ. This is the Father who, being the Mystery of the Beginning without beginning, the Fount of Life, cannot simply be Father but must be both Father and Mother.

> If the Son comes only from the Father, then this event must be considered both begetting and birth. There is here a significant change in the understanding of the Father. A father that both begets a son and brings him into the world cannot simply be a father, but must be a maternal father. God is both the maternal father of his only begotten son and the paternal mother of her only child.[45]

The Church took the same stance on this issue in the XIth Council of Toledo in 675 A.D.:

> . . . we must believe that the Son did not come from nothing nor from any other substance, but he was begotten or born *(genitus vel natus)* from the maternal womb of the Father *(de utero Patris).*

Here, without recourse to patriarchal categories, the wisdom of the Church rose above both patriarchal monotheism and matriarchal pantheism, while at the same time eschewing any earth-heaven dualism. The Christian trinitarian doctrine, and its affirmations of the mystery of the Abba of Jesus as maternal Father and paternal Mother, opens the way for the formation of a community of men and women which, "in the fellowship of the Holy Spirit" (II Cor. 13:13), should proceed to overcome privilege and domination of every sort.

The Maternal Father of Jesus also permits us to overcome the body-soul dualism. The God conceived in a patriarchal key is distant and sovereign, invulnerable to the sorrows and suffering of humanity, silent before the cross of his Son, which endures in history. In contrast, the Abba of Jesus, the Mystery of life, who both begets and gives birth, participates and is passionately involved in the sufferings of the people of Israel. This God dwells among the humble and lowly through his *Shekinah* who accompanies the children of Jacob into exile.[46]

In the Passion of the Son the Father attains the maximum point of universal openness. In delivering the beloved Son, begotten and born from all eternity, into the hands of men to be crucified, the Abba is also delivered over to suffer in the divine womb of the maternal Father, the infinite sorrow, the anguished impotence, the death of his maternal fatherhood. However, at the same time and in the same unique movement of trinitarian love, the passion of God who is maternal Father, who is Son, who is Spirit of love, opens wide the gates of salvation to all the abandoned of this world.

> Our release from pain and our deliverance from suffering spring from the suffering of the whole Trinity: from the death of the Son, the grief of the Father, and the patient endurance of the Spirit. God sets us free to live through his suffering love.[47]

In the Passion of his Son, the maternal Father and the Spirit of Love join with those who have to learn, living and suffering, to be human beings in agapic community. In the Passion of trinitarian love is the best integration and redemption of all aspects of human beings.

Conclusion: The Trinity as the Ultimate Possibility for Integrating the Masculine and the Feminine

With the progressive emergence of the feminine in nearly every other area of study today, theology faces a revolution in its own camp.

> The androcentric convergence of the Scriptural prism and its classical interpretation is fragmented into a million pieces. The disappearance of patriarchal structures implies a real revolution which affects all human language about God. It refers to a more profound paradigmatic change than ever before seen in the history of Christian doctrine.[48]

It seems that trinitarian theology may have a decisive role in this transformation. As a mystery which integrates into divine unity, pluralism, change, and difference, it is also capable of integrating, in a happy synthesis, the masculine and the feminine. It understands them in light of its first and last fundamental principle which is God. Trinitarian theology in this way affects not only human verbalization about the divine, but also the larger symbolic order.

In relationship to anthropology and the concept of God: If the divine image is found in women as well as in men, if the God we believe in has traits and ways of behaving that are as much masculine as feminine, then in order to describe God it will be necessary from now on to use words, metaphors, and images that are masculine and feminine. If women as well as men are *theomorphous,* that is, made in the image of God, it is imperative that this God in whose image they appear no longer be described or thought of as simply andromorphous but as *anthropomorphous.*[49] We know that we will have to struggle with the poverty of human language—limited as it is to express the majesty and ineffability of the divine. Meanwhile, in attempting to include all of humanity, the combination of the two symbols, two languages, and the two metaphors—masculine and feminine—gives us more to work with in portraying the divine.

In respect to societal structure and social relationships: Basically, the trinitarian mystery of God is a mystery of the community; it has social implications. For this reason, a lone individual cannot be the image of this God except insofar as he or she is open to relationship and communitarian being. This has direct consequences for our theme and its relevance in Latin America today. A society in which the poor and needy are excluded and marginalized cannot be said to bear the seeds of the Kingdom which Jesus proclaimed nor can it possibly be even a shadow of the social image of the Triune God. In the same way, a society in which women have an inferior status and are not partners with men in the struggle for justice and in the attempt to live as friends is also far from representing the trinitarian mystery of God.

The Fathers of the Church saw an analogy and the image of God in three persons in the original nuclear family: Adam, Eve, and Seth.[50] In spite of all the problems and limitations of this analogy it allows for some insights which may give us a better understanding of human relations. The human family as image of God, shows us that God is the mystery of love—and a fruitful love—and that God's trinitarian being is not closed in on itself but is fulfilled by surrendering itself and giving itself freely out of the richness of its immanent being. Moreover, if the woman, man, and child are images of God on earth, then eternal paternity, maternity, and infancy are revealed to us in the Triune God.[51] Femininity and infancy, then, have an assured place in the divine mystery.

Most importantly, this view allows true masculinity to be seen in its original dignity, without the deforming marks of patriarchal domination. It also rids us of body-soul dualism, since the body and everything pertaining to it is reintegrated into the glory of God's image. The total human person—man, woman, and child, in body and in spirit—is the image of God on earth. The body can be the temple of the Holy Spirit because it is the intelligible image of God in the world.

Furthermore, this view suggests that human and social relationships shouldn't be defined only in terms of efficacy and activity that can easily degenerate into desire for power and obsessive pragmatism. Instead, they should harmoniously balance the most "feminine" characteristics of *grace* and receptivity, and the most "childlike" characteristics of purity and trust. This social doctrine of the Trinity, as it integrates without suppressing the divine differences in an agapic unity of love, allows us to find a theological basis for building a "social personalism" or a "personal socialism"[52] as an alternative to our present society.

Trinitarian theology and the rediscovery of its feminine traits has—as we have tried to demonstrate here—its basis in the Holy Scriptures and in the traditions of the Church. For this reason, it is inscribed in the heart of a people who can count on the constant companionship of a God who desires liberation from all kinds of oppression. The Church in Latin America today, the Church that has made a preferential option for the oppressed, proclaims the God of life. This God is a strong, protective Father and at the same time a loving, eternal Mother. The human image of this God is found within the community of liberated men and women who, side by side, are building the kingdom of God. They hope and pray for the promised time when all domination, whether patriarchal or matriarchal, will be overcome, and a future day will know neither lords nor slaves. In the messianic humanity there is "neither Jew nor Greek, neither slave nor free, neither male nor female" (Gal. 3:28). In Latin America today, we are called to construct such humanity from, and find its destination in, the great mystery of Love, which we call Father, Son, and Holy Spirit, which, in its infinite mercy, is revealed both as a generative and a creative force, and as a womb that gives birth and stirs with compassion.

5

Women and Christology

Nelly Ritchie

Any theo-logy must hold that Jesus is God. Liberation christology emphasizes that we only know what God is from a point of departure in Jesus. This, I maintain, is the kernel of our Christian faith, which is at once the Good News and a scandal.[1]

—Jon Sobrino

"Who do you say that I am?" (Mark 8:29). . . . The answer Christians give to this everlastingly historical question is always a historical one, since believers are themselves historical.[2]

Because we accept the historicity of the questions as well as the answers, we believe that it is important to tell a little about our own situation as Latin American women. Our particular situation influences the question. What we do about it influences the answers.

In addition to accepting this historicity—that of questions and

---

Translated from the Spanish by Jeltje Aukema.

answers—we must be aware of the provisional nature of certain affirmations. We are less concerned about the veracity of these affirmations—which do not depend on absolutes—than about the reality out of which they arise.

We aim here to redeem the permanent: life, justice, grace, salvation, freedom, pardon, etc. In the midst of historical conflict these things will change, or will change us—if we have an attitude of honest, genuine searching—in as much as we know how to distinguish God's permanent offer of salvation from the passing (yet valid) responses of humankind.

The statement: Jesus is the Christ! covers new dimensions. It does not have to do with an applied doctrine but with a truth to discover, with a response which, translated into words and deeds, takes on historical truthfulness and liberating force.

The affirmation: The Christ is Jesus! will lead us to new historical commitments with the God revealed in Jesus of Nazareth, and with the project which he unveils with the inauguration of his Kingdom.

Talking about Christology means trying to match that which is relative to:

Messiah → Jesus Christ: God revealed and made manifest in the midst of historical conflict.

Savior → the one who incarnates God's plan to liberate humanity.

Lord → the one who calls people to be active participants in their own liberation; the response to this call means active participation in the already inaugurated Kingdom of God.

This attempt to give answers happens within our context as Latin American women. Ours is a situation which—as we have said before—influences the questions and answers, and must be examined in depth. This is the only way we can engage in a truly fruitful dialogue with the Word of God. The rereading—that is, the reading of the text from our particular context—will encourage our search by presenting us with new responses and provoking new questions.

Our Reality As:

Women

Every day we are confronted with what others expect of us and with what we really want to be. We search for new alternative models for action. We rebel against structures that limit, oppress, and deny our self-realization. As women in search of new forms of co-operation, solidarity, and life, we discover the need to organize ourselves and to join with others in order to combine forces and resist whatever tries to limit human freedom and dignity. We find that in order to be able to confront oppressive structures we must reject individualistic schemes.

Latin Americans

This term does not signify only a geographic designation and a common history; it refers to a painful and alienating reality. This is a contradictory reality of a subjugated, dominated, exploited, fighting, and yet hopeful continent that is bleeding to death. It is the reality of people impoverished by enemies from without and within.

This is why we as Latin American women do not talk of our own private liberation but of the liberation of our people. The reality of our people includes and transcends our personal histories. For us, liberation in male-female relationships will take place within Latin American liberation; it will be a continent-wide project that does not overlook all our regional peculiarities.

Thus, we can speak of Latin America as the motherland who links us, who brings us together, and encourages us in the search for an integrated future, a future in which we can realize our dream of breaking down the barriers that others raise between us.

Christians

This is not a "religious" epithet; rather, it is a cosmic vision. It is indicative of the motives and basis of our struggle and of our efforts. As the Incarnate Word, Jesus Christ is God's revealed word. We fight against any use of this word to disguise reality. Instead we promote a dialogical and transformative word that uncovers this reality.[3] We already are—in hope!—a people of equals. But we want to be able to anticipate this plan in our time, in our part of the world. We want to make it a reality in history and to be protagonists of this process.

Our reality means that we are women, we belong to Latin America, and we are members of the body of Christ. We are setting out on an adventure which will bring together all our humble contributions. We do so with the confidence that together we will enrich each other's lives, we will inspire one another, and share the work involved in liberating our continent.

What follows is our attempt to dialogue, from our reality, with the reality of the Word of God. That is the search for those lines of action that enrich this transforming dialogue. These lines lead us from reality——to the Word of God, from the light of the Word ——to transforming action and then back again——to a rereading of the Bible.

We have chosen the book of Luke for this dialogue. We have a good reason for this choice. The author of Luke was obviously very concerned about the poor of his time; he refers to the sick, marginalized, children, and women. This emphasis leads to a particular christological view which enriches our task in Latin America in a special way.

Our effort does not stem from, nor will it end in, doctrinal statements; nor is it our goal to "apply" known christological titles to our reality. What we hope to do is to provoke new questions and to open ourselves up to the marvelous revelations of God who, in Jesus, is shown to be the Liberator.

> The historical Jesus is being recovered in Latin America lest in Christ's name the coexistence of the misery of reality and the Christian faith be acceptable or even justifiable. Or positively: the purpose of the recovery of the historical Jesus in Latin America is that salvation history be historical salvation.[4]

Jesus: The Christ of Life

Woman, don't cry.

A woman mourning the death of her son. This is not a rare occurence in Latin America. Here young people are cut down every day by aggression, repression, or simply the lack of opportunities. In Argentina, one woman, many women crying for their missing children, became symbols of women's resistance to the state terrorism which, for more than seven years, marked the darkest chapter of our country's history. The Mothers of the Plaza del Mayo are a symbol of the courageous struggle of women who chose to confront the powers of death. They risked their own lives in trying to reclaim the lives of those to whom they had given life. Their struggle extended to and was in solidarity with all the "other children."

> When a mother comes looking for help, without holding back, we offer her what we have. Above all, we protect life . . . we don't only look for our own children . . . we search for all those who are missing. We have made the broadest possible commitment to our people to protect life, justice, and freedom. What we are doing is not only looking back at the past, but also toward the future. . . . When they take a child away from a woman, they also take away her fear. I have found that the most beautiful way to die is to die for a cause.[5]

There are others who, from a supposedly Christian position, have organized around this cause and who try to ignore or silence these cries—or even worse, try to justify the disappearances and deaths.

Luke 7:12–15

> When he was near the gate of the town it happened that a dead man was being carried out for burial, the only son of his mother, and she was a widow. And a considerable number of the townspeople were with her. When the Lord saw her he felt sorry for her. "Do not cry," he said. Then he

went up and put his hand on the bier and the bearers stood still, and he said, "Young man, I tell you to get up." And the dead man sat up and began to talk, and Jesus *gave him to his mother*.

Let us look more closely for a moment at this scene: a woman has just lost her only company and support. God stands still before such human agony and is moved. Each time the Gospel speaks of Jesus' suffering compassion, it shows his complete identification with the other's situation; it shows his creative and active solidarity. Jesus' feelings precipitate changes—a search for the causes—that transform the pain-causing situation.

This ability to "feel with others" leads Jesus to stop hunger, eradicate illness, and remove the burdens that hamper life. His compassion does not stop with saying "Don't cry" but goes on to restore what the person has lost so that tears are replaced by true joy.

Woman→ "Don't cry"→Young Man→ "Get up!"

Resurrection, the giving back of life, like a miracle, is a sign that anticipates the complete transformation for which Christ is responsible. By what he did, Jesus Christ let the "recipients" and the witnesses of his action know that God restores life and defeats death. All of us who proclaim the Lordship of Jesus Christ are called to "Get up!" and to speak of this God who passes judgment on those who claim power over others' lives. We are called to be in solidarity with those who cry and search, to help restore what is lost to those who mourn.

To be witnesses of the resurrection means to refute the final triumph of death; it means to fight against all that limits abundant life. To be witnesses to the new life means to proclaim and build new roads of hope in the face of the hopelessness and bitterness of the defeated.

When we read about life in the early Church (according to the Acts of the Apostles), we discover that faith was shared with joy because it was more than a message of the triumph of life over death. It was an actual experience of fraternal community; in the sharing of the loaves and fishes, their eyes were opened to faith. It also meant not suffering from need because this new life—the experience of the resurrection—was a "kerygmatic" life, and the community was a "sign."

Jesus: The Christ of Grace

Woman, your faith has made you whole, go in peace.

Nothing separates us from God like a piety that is sure of itself. Nothing draws us closer to God than acknowledgement of the grace of pardon, the offer of a new chance for abundant grace.

> The ultimate language of faith is love. Those who would verify their own truth concerning the Christ will in the last resort have to question themselves about their love for Christ.[6]

Let's look for a moment at the following passage.

> One of the Pharisees invited him to a meal. When he arrived at the Pharisee's house and took his place at table, a woman came in, who had a bad name in the town. She had heard he was dining with the Pharisee and had brought with her an alabaster jar of ointment. She waited behind him at his feet, weeping, and her tears fell on his feet, and she wiped them away with her hair; then she covered his feet with kisses and anointed them with the ointment.
>
> When the Pharisee who had invited him saw this, he said to himself, "If this man were a prophet, he would know who this woman is that is touching him and what a bad name she has." Then Jesus took him up and said, "Simon, I have something to say to you." "Speak, Master" was the reply. "There was once a creditor who had two men in his debt; one owed him five hundred denarii, the other fifty. They were unable to pay, so he pardoned them both. Which of them will love him more?" "The one who was pardoned more, I suppose" answered Simon. Jesus said, "You are right."
>
> Then he turned to the woman. "Simon," he said "you see this woman? I came into your house, and you poured no water over my feet, but she has poured out her tears over my feet

> and wiped them away with her hair. You gave me no kiss, but she has been covering my feet with kisses ever since I came in. You did not anoint my head with oil, but she has anointed my feet with ointment. For this reason I tell you that her sins, her many sins, must have been forgiven her, or she would not have shown such great love. It is the man who is forgiven little who shows little love." Then he said to her, "Your sins are forgiven." Those who were with him at table began to say to themselves, "Who is this man, that he even forgives sins?" But he said to the woman, "Your faith has saved you; go in peace" (Luke 7:36–50).

Jesus consistently refuses to recognize the claims of those who think they have "earned" their salvation, particularly those who base their claims on their having perfectly kept the law—including the commandment about love. This is why he often uses the image of the slave or the "least of these;" he even refers to himself as "servant" (Cf. John 13).

Not only did Jesus proclaim the good news of salvation and announce with his coming that the Kingdom was at hand and that the Jubilee Year had begun, but his acts of love and forgiveness substantiated his message. All of his acts were historically inclusive: the healings, breaking bread with the marginalized, spending time with beggars, and so forth. These acts speak of a new period of grace where:

- those who are sure of their piety are scandalized,
- the dispossessed are happy and the hungry are filled with good things.

We are reminded of the woman who came to Jesus: she was a social outcast, condemned and marginalized. She was for Jesus—the Christ—someone who was not afraid to let others know how she felt, who loved unconditionally, who offered what she had, and who anointed him with her life. She had already been admitted—perhaps without knowing it—into the presence of grace.

> Grace is not something mysterious in the sense of being impalpable. Grace is the personal, living presence of God in life itself, dwelling there to make it more fully life . . .[7]

Only the person who can love without reservation can reach this dimension.

> This was Christ's revelation. To be saved is to reach the fullness of love; it is to enter into the circle of charity which unites the three Persons of the Trinity; it is to love as God loves.[8]

Jesus' words explain the woman's loving and gratuitous act. In doing so, he assures her acceptance into the new community where her debt is settled and she is welcomed into the Kingdom. It is a Kingdom where:

- the weak are strengthened,
- the poor receive the Good News,
- the eyes of the blind are opened, the deaf hear and the lame walk,
- and where the year of the Lord's favor is proclaimed (Cf. Luke 4:18–19).

This new time of grace is full of joy and hope. Forgiveness restores us, grace is a gift, love is the language of solidarity.

Jesus: The Liberator Christ

Woman, I liberate you!

On the back streets of Latin America we find women with their "burdens":

- the peasant woman, stooped over the earth from which she must eke out a living for herself and her children.
- the woman who from the early hours of the morning is seen carrying tubs of water, washing clothes . . . carrying children.
- the homemaker trying to respond to all the needs of her loved ones, doing work that goes unrecognized.

The peasant woman, worker, homemaker, and we could mention many other women who know little of rest, who live in small worlds that use up their energies and leave them desperate. These women cannot manage to plan for the future because they barely have strength to get through today. These are women who are burdened with double exploitation: for belonging to our oppressed peoples and for being women. Many of them turn to religion looking for an escape or to alleviate the pain of their situation, only to be confronted with rationalizations that increase their burdens.

Luke 13:10–17

> One sabbath day he [Jesus] was teaching in one of the synagogues, and a woman was there who for eighteen years had been possessed by a spirit that left her enfeebled; she was bent double and quite unable to stand upright. When Jesus saw her he called her over and said, "Woman, you are rid of your infirmity" and he laid his hands on her. And at once she straightened up, and she glorified God.
>
> But the synagogue official was indignant because Jesus had healed on the sabbath, and he addressed the people present. "There are six days," he said, "when work is to be done. Come and be healed on one of those days and not on the sabbath." But the Lord answered him. "Hypocrites!" he said. "Is there one of you who does not untie his ox or his donkey from the manger on the sabbath and take it out for watering? And this woman, a daughter of Abraham whom Satan has held bound for these eighteen years—was it not right to untie her bonds on the sabbath day?" When he said this, all his adversaries were covered with confusion, and all the people were overjoyed at all the wonders he worked.

According to the Gospel of Luke, this is the last time Jesus went into a synagogue before his journey to the cross. Here, he confronted institutionalized religion. It was appropriate for him to draw our attention to the situation with which this burdened and bent-over woman was confronted. This is not the only time that Jesus criticised the religious leadership for being hypocrites, placing burdens on others which they would not carry themselves. On this occasion an act of Jesus became:

- an act of judgment on the establishment,
- and an act of liberation for a burdened woman.

Jesus' judgment falls on those leaders who claim to serve and honor God but who show little regard for humanity.

> It is not enough to say that love of God is inseparable from the love of one's neighbor. It must be added love for God is unavoidably expressed *through* love of one's neighbor. Moreover, God is loved in the neighbor.[9]

This is revealed in the health that casts off the burden. In light of this, the day of rest will regain its originally intended purpose (the overburdened do not receive such rest days), and liberation opens a new path:

- where people can look ahead to the future,
- where there is a broader horizon of action and creation,
- where it is possible for joy to be shared among the people ("the multitudes were made joyful"),
- where it is possible to rest because it is possible to act.

Jesus, the Christ, reveals the constancy and persistence of God's project of liberation. In God this liberation is made action and this act is valuable in itself because it defers to a greater reality:

> The liberation of Jesus takes on a double aspect: on the one hand it proclaims the liberation of all of history . . . on the other it anticipates the totality in a process that is concretized in partial liberations always open to the totality.[10]

Jesus: The Christ of the Kingdom

Militant woman, "you have chosen the better part . . ."

Below you will find transcriptions I have written of testimonies of Argentinian women who from various backgrounds have committed themselves to, and continue in, the struggle for dignity and human rights.[11]

Delia Boschi de Blanco, who works for the Telephone Company, says:

. . . and I would draw extra special attention to what working women, mostly mothers and homemakers, have done for their situation as workers. We note that there are 500 million women working to help make the world rich. They represent a third of the salaried work force in the world.

This irreversible social phenomenon is constantly changing. It plays an enormous role in the struggles of the working class, of which we are a part, as well as of society as a whole. . . . There is a large percentage of women in all of the guilds. During the years of the dictatorship, we were out in the streets waving banners along with other popular organizations; we demonstrated for freedom, against the repression, for the reinstatement of fired workers, for those who had been disappeared, for the release of political prisoners. . . . Even after showing that we are able to lead, we are still discriminated against. There are only seven women representing us in the government, and not one single minister . . . to say nothing of the unions. . . . The success of the general demands of the working class and in particular of working women . . . depends on whether the unions are able to operate as freely as unions should. . . . This is a form of being on the offensive in getting our particular demands met, as well as those of the people as a whole.

Susana Pírez Gallart, Vice President of the Executive Board of the Permanent Assembly for Human Rights says:

Women must assume their responsibilities as citizens. Each woman must do her part. Political activity doesn't only mean belonging to a political party. Being politically active also means belonging to a neighborhood center, a co-operative, a professional or cultural association, a guild, to whatever. It is necessary to be supportive because the foundation of a democracy is freedom of association, and because democracy can't be static. Democracy must be dynamic, it must be active. . . . Only when women become active in this struggle for liberation in large numbers will they make a place for themselves. Then they will be able to have a real part in the struggle for national liberation.

Señora Graciela Fernandez Meijide, another human rights worker, states:

> . . . women were not repressed for being women but for having dared to stray from their role and take on a new one. They were repressed for having taken up the struggle along side men for the rights that were justly theirs. However, women have been particularly vulnerable in torture situations. They have been attacked in horribly sadistic ways. Perhaps in revenge for their having dared to stand up for themselves. Not only have they themselves been vulnerable but through their children they have been doubly vulnerable. When a woman is detained, her children are detained with her. It is even worse for the woman who is pregnant when she is detained because they often beat her so badly that she loses her child.

The life of the woman who "dares" (to use Graciela's words) is difficult. She is confronted with a reality that subjects, denigrates, and marginalizes her; and she rebels against it. She does not accept "the givens" as absolutes, as things that cannot be changed. Yet, she dares to act, participate, and demand a life of dignity that allows hope. This option, the choice to belong, is what the Gospel refers to when it talks about "the better part" which Jesus said "is not to be taken from her." Let's read the following stories together.

Felicidad Abadí a Crespo and her sister Dominga worked in the Lozadur factory. One of the two was a manager. There was a conflict because of problems between the management and the employees and the union. The negotiator threatened the workers and the union leaders at the meeting.

In the course of their journey he came to a village, and a woman named Martha welcomed him into her house. She had a sister called Mary, who sat down at the Lord's feet and listened to him speaking. Now Martha who was distracted with all the serving said, "Lord, do you

> He told them to tell their colleagues to stop their complaining or they would be sorry. After the meeting, both of the women were fired. A few days later the army tore their house apart and took them away. We never saw them again . . . Felicidad and Dominga were disappeared for defending their rights as workers (From Graciela Meijide's story).

> not care that my sister is leaving me to do the serving all by myself? Please tell her to help me." But the Lord answered: "Martha, Martha," he said "you worry and fret about so many things, and yet few are needed, indeed only one. It is Mary who has chosen the better part; it is not to be taken from her" (Luke 10:38–42).

Choosing to commit oneself to the people's struggle, to the search for life for all, or to dedicate oneself to a cause is, from our faith perspective, the way to proclaim the lordship of Christ over all other lords. Putting ourselves "at his feet," as the text says, as disciples, following him and volunteering to serve the cause of the Kingdom, leads us to find the Lord. We meet him in the midst of the pain, the struggle, the strength, and the hope of those—victims of injustice—who devote themselves to the cause of justice. This is to choose "the better part that will not be taken away" from us because it is God's own cause.

Socially acceptable "activism"—like Martha's—contrasts with Mary's position of defiance which dares to proclaim with action that which is completely new in Jesus. Mary's decision and her action are a christological statement.

> Behind the announcement of the "Kingdom," that is, of the new social and political reality that is ready to be built in the land of Israel, behind the certainty that history is propelled by an invisible Lord who created the people and called his prophets, is found the construction of this society of new human beings that will live according to revolutionary criteria, that will give women the same position of dignity and responsibility as that of men. . . . These are the germs of a human and cultural revolution that began in that time (and

was promptly stopped) and that from time to time reappears . . .[12]

New Questions

By way of conclusion . . .

If we accept our reality as the point of departure, if dialogue with the Word of God and especially with the Word Incarnate, Jesus Christ, sheds light on our analysis and gives us the strength for commitment, then we can return to our reality with some answers. Our eyes will be wide open to see the signs of the times, the newly revealed signs, and our ears will be alert to hear the new questions, the new cries, demands.

We would like to end with a quote from the apostle Paul which is more than a conclusion. This quote is an ancient christological hymn which reveals "who it is" that encourages and supports us on our journey.

> Let Christ be our example as to what our attitude should be. For he, who had always been God by nature, did not cling to his prerogatives as God's equal, but stripped himself of all privilege by consenting to be a servant and to be born as a human being. He became one of us. His surrender of love was a complete sacrifice. He did not run from pain nor was he afraid of the cross. He followed through to the end. For this reason, he did not die but was given new life by the Father. A new world is being born because of his resurrection. This is why we, Jesus' sisters, do not fold up our banners, nor are we afraid to join in the struggle. True life is born out of liberating surrender (Phil. 2:5–11).[13]

6

Women and the People of God

Aracely de Rocchietti

This essay represents a process of reflection on the Church in Latin America from the standpoint of a woman who, like many of her generation, finds herself living through a period of intense activity and reflection in the midst of profound wretchedness and astounding hope. This wretchedness dogs our lives and wipes the smiles off our faces. It invalidates the efforts we make, confronted as we are every day in Latin America with widespread injustice, martyrdom, and violation of our rights. It is a wretchedness of impotence in the face of the destruction of the lives to which we ourselves have given birth—lives which seek to grow up protected by the older generation, who enabled them to see the light of day but cannot give them support, security, rights, and liberty. It is a wretchedness in the face of the despotism of the political and economic empires which are bleeding us to death and—why should we conceal it?—in the face, too, of many of our Latin American brothers who are betraying us.

At the same time there is hope: the hope generated by belief in life and in the power to resist and to be creative, which God has

---

Translated from the Spanish by James C. G. Grieg.

given us to conquer death. It is the hope generated by belief in justice as an historical constant which reveals to us both God's love for all of creation and the human capacity to proclaim this and defend it. It is the hope that we may experience each day solidarity in the quest for survival and in the struggle for liberty—a solidarity which goes so far as the giving of one's life wholly in selfless surrender for others, thus reproducing many times over the example set by Christ.

Together, these two dimensions, wretchedness and hope, run through the analysis and the suggestions made in this essay, which is an attempt to reinterpret our Church experience as the People of God in biblical and theological terms. This is a theme which we consider to be fundamental, realizing that *to be* the People of God in *current* Latin American history is what gives the Church of Christ both its mandate and its *raison d'être*.

Without the dynamic of a people living and on the move as the embodiment of our whole continent's struggle for liberation, the Church cannot be a sign and witness to the Kingdom inaugurated by Jesus; nor will it be on the road to full self-realization, in which all the Utopian efforts to give dignity and liberation to human beings will be crowned with success. It is not the purpose of this essay to set woman apart on a pedestal in analyzing a situation in which I believe the really important distinction to be that between oppressors and oppressed. But since sexual oppression is, in its own way, part and parcel of the oppression of our peoples, I shall highlight the significance and the roles of women—in society and particularly in the Church—which have been ignored or obscured by biased and discriminating male-oriented approaches.

I have said that this is a reflection which is an ongoing process; and fundamentally that is true, because we are not accustomed to thinking from our own standpoint and holding opinions in defense of our rights. Even more seriously, we are not very well equipped for making an original analysis of our own. Rather, we depend on assumptions and models propounded by those who traditionally have the power and the means of thinking, and of publishing and dominating thought.

However, new fields are opening up and it is therefore useful that the work we are doing should be an ongoing process, so that we may be ready to look squarely at our thoughts and have an indepth dialogue—correcting each other in love and patience and, above all, being prepared to pursue humbly together, and with our comrades, a new course of action and reflection to which, with due acknowledgement of each other, we may contribute our efforts.

The Church: The People of God

An Approach to the Idea of the People of God from the Standpoint of Biblical Theology

When we have discussions about the nature and mission of the Church, especially on the ecumenical level, certain basic difficulties arise in our common understanding. Either the approach puts more emphasis on the character of the Church as the community of salvation (*People* λασζ*:* Tit. 2:14; Heb. 2:17; 1 Pet. 2:9; *Flock/Shepherd:* Matt. 26:31; Luke 12:32; Acts 20: 28 ff.; "whose shepherd is Christ": John 10:11–16; Heb. 13:20; *City* or *New Jerusalem:* Rev. 21:2; 21:9; *House* or *Temple of God:* 1 Tim. 3:25; Heb. 3:6, 10:21; 1 Pet. 4:17) or else the emphasis falls on the Church as a *Μυστŕριον* or covenant, the people of the Old Testament covenant (Gen. 9:1–17; Gen. 17:3–14; Exod. 24: 1–11, Jos. 24: 7–28),

> . . . a type (1 Cor. 10:6) of the true Israel of God and even of the whole of mankind which is set free from the slavery of sin and death through the blood of Christ and which has already entered into the "Sabbath rest" of God (Heb. 4:10ff.) on the strength of rebirth by the water of baptism and may taste of "the heavenly gift" (6:4). On the grounds of the contrast with "the Israel according to the flesh" (Gal. 4:22ff.; 1 Cor. 10–18) we may conclude that the Christian people is "the Israel according to the Spirit" (Eph. 2:12; Heb. 8:8–10; Rev. 7:4; 21:23).[1]

The Vine: Matt. 20:11–16; Rev. 14:17–20; *Bride/Groom:* 2 Cor. 11:2; Eph. 5:22–23; *Body/Head:* Eph. 5:28, related to the idea of a wife as the body of the husband, I Cor. 12:12; Rom. 12:4; a unit of the two gifts, Rom. 12:5; Eph. 1:22; 4:15; the *body* of Christ with him as the head.

This multiplicity of images and figures gives us a wide framework for getting close to the true meaning of the Church as an objective reality which permits us to analyze our own reality. If we start from the proclamation of Jesus, we find that given his sense of urgency as regards ". . . the end in a short (indeed a very short) time, he could not have thought of founding a church."[2]

On the other hand, the absence of the word ʾεκκλεσια from the Gospels (the two quotations of Matt. 16:18 and 18:17 surely reflect the language of the primitive Church), the problem of its interpretation as a universal Church or private community, and also the possibility that we try to give the name ʾεκκλεσια to the organization we find after the death of Christ, are all points which show us that it would be an anachronism to think Christ intended to found some stable community similar to what we know today as the Church. However, the material we find in the teaching of Jesus on the idea of the People of God is very full and rich.

Before we actually begin to describe Jesus' references to the People of God, I want to indicate that out of the hundred times when the word ʾεκκλεσια appears in the LXX, on seventy-two occasions it translates *qahal* or *qahal yahweh,* or "People of God" *ʾεκκλεσια:* Deut. 23: 1–3 and 8; 1 Chron. 28:3 cf.; Num. 16:3; 30:4 (a community of worship and salvation gathered before Yahweh).

Jesus constantly speaks about *a new people of God* gathered by him. "Indeed, we must put the point even more sharply: the *only* significance of the whole of Jesus' activity is to gather the eschatological people of God."[3]

Jesus uses rich images to refer to this new people, e.g., *flock* (Matt. 26:31ff.; John 10:1–29; Luke 10:3; Luke 11:23)—it is a flock which a shepherd gathers, brings together, and defends from the dangers of being scattered; *guests invited to a wedding* (Mark 2:19); a *fishing net* (Matt. 13:47); it is *built by God* (Matt. 16:28) or is the *city of God* set on Mount Zion (Matt. 5:14); or members of the New Covenant (Mark 14:24) in whom are fulfilled the promises made to the fathers; *the family of God,* an eschatological family whose father is God (Matt. 23:9), in which the correlative ideas appear of brothers (Mark 3:34) and the table-fellowship of the family. We shall come back very shortly to this idea as it is a key for understanding the new and revolutionary call of Jesus to the People of God.

All the ideas mentioned above reveal a will to gather the New

People, which is also implicit in other similar efforts in the Judaism of Jesus' day. In particular, the Pharisees and the Essenes were responsible for these endeavors, of which, however, the basic philosophy was the idea of a holy remnant interpreted on strict lines as an exclusive group, with stringent religious and ethical regulations for those who were to be members of it.

Very closely related to the preaching of the remnant was John the Baptist. He gives his preaching a new perspective, more faithful to the message of the Prophets. With his emphasis on penitence and repentance he calls a remnant which includes sinners ready to go through the experience of conversion (Luke 3:7–14). This unrestricted remnant is the herald of the new people which we shall see later in Acts and in Paul as the community of the redeemed in Christ (1 Cor. 12:28, Col. 1:18–24).

Jesus does not basically reject the idea of calling groups of people and gathering them together. In fact, in his turn, he gathers a small group and in the movement of his followers some similarity with the Essenes can also be found: the renunciation of property, the forbidding of oaths and identification by common prayer; but it is very important to note that Jesus *violently rejects* the idea of separating that group from the community. Jesus calls together a community in which there is a place for those who are of no account, those who are rejected because of their physical defects, their sex or their race. Jesus rejected the idea of creating a restricted, separate, and sanctified community.

Jesus announces limitless grace and calls even his own people to repentance. He shows that the division is not between the people of Israel and other peoples but between those who, having been called, respond, and those who do not.

> The work of Christ is presented simultaneously as a liberation from sin and all its consequences: despoliation, injustice, hatred. This liberation fulfills in an unexpected way the promises of the prophets and creates a new chosen people, which this time includes all humanity.[4]

This new community comes into existence within a new relationship to God, a new relationship which breaks the bonds of the earthly family and so points toward a new model of a wider family open to all those ready to respond to the call of that Father whose goodness is unlimited.

> Wherever people are won over by the good news and join company with the new People of God, they leave the world of death for the world of life (Matt. 8:22 par. Luke 9:60; John 5:24; cf. Luke 15:24, 32). Now they belong under the reign of God; a new life is beginning which consists of a new relationship to God and a new relationship to man.[5]

The all-inclusive element of this community must not, however, make us underrate the responsibilities and the demands. Jesus preaches with clarity a new relation between humanity and God and between men and women under the grace of this new relationship which is already to be found among his disciples as the eschatological gift of salvation. The condition of Sonship is consummated in the framework of the Kingdom. Meanwhile, this new community moves forward in the certainty of future salvation, a certainty which is the expression of God's purpose of salvation for all humanity (Matt. 18:10); confidence in the midst of daily life (Matt. 6:8–32); courage in face of suffering (Matt. 5:11); and also in the demands which we see clearly in the six antitheses of the Sermon on the Mount, which go beyond the old law, i.e., reconciliation with one's brethren (Matt. 5:21–26); the new attitude in regard to women (Matt. 5:27–30), to divorce (Matt. 5:31–32), and to oaths (Matt. 5:33–37); the attitude toward one's enemies (Matt. 5:38–42), a passive attitude, and in 43–48 an active attitude. These postulates are a call to a discipline for life, the most important points in which are: the sanctification of everyday life; greetings; humility; discipline in the use of words; common prayer; renunciation of property—*not however as a personal merit of holiness and separateness, but as a communal discipline* for life through love for the other and faithfulness to God.

This idea of a new people, a people open to the action of God—a people inclusive enough to be for the poor, for women, children, the disabled, Jews, and Gentiles—did not make itself apparent in *any great expansion of this new people,* which remained a minority and, in a certain way, exclusive. The demands of the call left many by the roadside; cf. the parable of the Sower. But that was not all.

According to theologian Juan Luis Segundo, the special features of the incarnation of Christianity in the very history of humanity are, in themselves, a great limitation.

> In the early days of Christianity, Saint Paul was asked to explain who he was in terms of religion. In his answer, he felt obliged to acknowledge the smallness and insignificance of the nascent Church: "This much I will admit: I am a follower of the new way (the 'sect' they speak of), and it is in that manner that I worship the God of our fathers" (Acts 24:14). . . . The Church follows in the footsteps of Jesus, its founder and God-made-man. The limitation of the Church, then, is not so much the result of its unworthiness as the result of its incarnation.[6]

Some Approaches for Our Rereading and Analysis of the Church's Situation in Latin America

The Church as the Mysterium and Community of Salvation

As regards the actual nature of the Church, it is important to bring into relief the two aspects which emerge from the biblical message:

The Church as a Mystery. Here we understand mystery as:

> . . . the eternal counsel and decision of God and the concrete revelation and actualisation of this counsel in the history of created reality as a whole and salvation history in particular . . . the church in its character as mystery is characterized as an essential factor in the carrying out of this counsel and decision.[7]

It follows that the Church has a function which it cannot abandon, as a sign and sacrament (a *particular* reality) and as an expression of the very mystery of Christ (the *universal* reality).

> The historical pageant of the "incarnate" Christ, prepared by the Old Testament and prolonged by the visible Church, em-

braces and manifests the mystery of God's unfolding plan for all humanity.[8]

The Church as a Community of Salvation. The Church as a mystery, as the body of Christ, becomes visible in its incarnation, and in its historical realization it assumes a defined sociological structure through which it is related to other social structures. The characteristics of this community of the called and its life as a brotherhood are described in I Peter 2:9 ff. and 2:17. It is a community of the unity of the Spirit (Eph. 4:2)—a community in which differences do not count (Gal. 3:28).

The Church as the People of God

Another approach I want to come back to is that of the Church as the new People of God, understood as explained in the previous point. But how is this people made up? Mark 16:15–16 suggests, "only those who believed and were baptized"; or, those who remain in the specific community; or again, in Matt. 25:32–46 ("As you did it to one of the least of these you did it to me"), those who have not recognized the Lord but who have expressed their solidarity with the gift of themselves and by their love for others—who have already had a foretaste of the gift of the Grace of God—will be saved.

Undoubtedly, salvation is a universal plan of God for all humanity. In this affirmation we accept the biblical theological interpretation presented above. And in this setting we discover the Church as the community which has received that universal salvation by revelation and *proclaims* it to the world. But even more than Christ did, it experiences and shares the first fruits of the new relationship with God in the meeting together of that new people (worship, solidarity, teaching).

The Absence of Institutional Models

Another approach I should like to highlight is the resistance of Jesus to providing a model or paradigm for this new community and to institutionalizing it, partly because for him time was limited and pressing but fundamentally because of an option for liberty and faithfulness which is a defense against temptations and worldly powers. This absence of models is compensated for by the diversity and wealth of images.

From the standpoint of the marginalized members of society, Jesus' steadfastness is seen in the clear indication that he rejected the creation of an exclusive and discriminatory community, and in his unquestionable solidarity and identification of himself with the marginalized, in his rehabilitation of the despised, his challenge to prejudice, and his confrontation with the institutionalized religion of the rich and powerful. The unmistakable universal nature in the changed composition of the New People is seen in the fact that access to them is by baptism and not by circumcision.

The life of Jesus itself manifests and fulfills the expectations of those poor members of society (Mary, Elizabeth, Zechariah, the shepherds) and at the same time is a threat to those who hold power and interpret the history of salvation in accordance with their own interests.

> Next day, that is, when Preparation Day was over, the chief priests and the Pharisees went in a body to Pilate and said to him, "Your Excellency, we recall that this impostor said, while he was still alive, 'After three days I shall rise again.' Therefore give the order to have the sepulcher kept secure until the third day, for fear his disciples come and steal him away and tell the people, 'He has risen from the dead.' This last piece of fraud would be worse than what went before" (Matt. 27:62–65).

I think it is highly important to continue analysis of that initial urge of Jesus to open up a new scenario for the marginalized—women among them—because that urge has been repeatedly distorted and lost sight of in the life of the Church. We must not forget that the Word of God was spoken by the people but *interpreted, thought, put into writing, and transmitted* by the powerful of all ages: learned doctors, scribes, priests, kings, fathers of the Church; that the life of the Church necessarily had to develop within the prevailing structures in which Jesus was someone who belonged to the "counter culture"; that from its start, the Church trying to proclaim the Gospel of Christ was assimilating structures of power which it ultimately came to adopt for its own institutional structure as it grew. This has meant that successive reinterpretations reflect wholly biased aspects of Jesus' understanding of that New People which we have to incarnate and rediscover from the reality of our own situation in faithfulness to God.

The Leading Role of Woman in the People of God

In Biblical Time (up to the Time of the Historical Jesus)

Traditionally, when we speak of woman in the People of God, we are looking for those situations (generally exceptional) in which various women take on a role or a ministry which has been mentioned in the pages of the written revelation. Or, again, we expect to see them as mothers, wives, or co-workers with great men. I think that if this approach is the only one, it does not allow us to read the situation in a more interesting way; it hides from us some aspects of status which, though not particularly striking, are nevertheless valid, and it does not tell us much about the absence of women or about their being ignored.

We are not greatly accustomed to "trying to see" salvation history from the standpoint of women—a particularly interesting angle, especially in the period of the historical Jesus. My question therefore is: How did women take Jesus' message? and not: How did Jesus regard these women? And this is why one can speak of women who have a leading role in the People of God—women who, absent or present, give us keys for interpreting and living out our faith.

When we think of women in the Hebrew Bible, we have to take into account that we have received an inheritance of scriptures which covers almost a thousand years of history in which there were different types of society: the patriarchs, the monarchy, and the society of post-exilic Judaism.

Without going into familiar detail for each period, we may say that woman figures in the people of Israel without having her position defined socially, legally, and in religious terms. She is defined in relation to man. To start with, she is the daughter of *X*, then she is the wife of *X*, then his mother (1 Sam. 18:17,19,27). Whether married or even just betrothed, her obligation was to be completely faithful to the man. She had no right to ask for a divorce but the husband could legally leave her—disgraced at that—if she failed to carry out all her duties (something shameful). What is more, it was a disgrace to be single or a virgin or barren (Gen. 30:19–23).

Woman was on a level with man as regards punishments (pain of death)—for adultery for instance—but not in the rights of inheritance, which give absolute priority to the men of the family (Num. 27:1–11). If raped while a virgin, an Israelite woman was dependent on negotiations between the man and her father, and these could end in marriage or simply in the payment of a marriage portion.

In religion, woman was excluded from all the ministries of worship. She took part in family religious ceremonies as part of the family gathered round the man. Resident strangers and workers were also included in the family.

If she became a mother, a woman had to refrain from touching any sacred objects and had to be in the sanctuary for a period of purification coinciding with her puerperium. And this period of purification was doubled if she gave birth to a daughter (Leviticus 12:1–8). She had to offer a sacrifice for *sin* and the priest would *purify* her by the expiation he offered.

Woman's role as mother is emphasized, but in relation to the importance of her sons for the revelation of God: Hagar, Rebecca, the mother of Moses, the mother of the Maccabees, Elizabeth and Mary.

The Bible's statements indicating another idea of woman are important, and we could regard them as the seeds of a different view of her:

- First of all, Chapters 1 and 2 of Genesis. Two points should be noted: *Man and woman* created in the image and likeness of God (Genesis 1:26), from the same substance with a difference which serves only to reaffirm their unity and not the hierarchical treatment or subjection of the one by the other; and secondly *the same commandment to both:* to multiply and have dominion over the world. These two missions are for both of them, without any division of responsibilites or labor.
- Deborah exemplifies a *recognized leadership* and we must not underrate the example. It belongs however to the period of the

charismatic judges. We do not find woman with power when it is transmitted within the categories of a society structured in accordance with genealogical descent and absolute masculine power.

There are no queens nor are there priestesses in Israel, and as we approach the revelation of which Jesus is the incarnation, the women *continue to be mothers of the men.* In Matthew's genealogy there is a clear indication of the Israelite descent of Jesus, and the women appear only as an outside influence (Matt. 1:3–6).

It can be seen that, basically, woman has a socially passive attitude as regards her freedom of decision, but not an anonymous one, for even in the highly prejudiced and circumscribed interpretation we receive from the written Revelation, woman is present, if perhaps obscured as to her real image and diminished in her importance—but present and active in those areas to which she was able to have access.

By Jesus' day, women's freedom had been restricted in various ways, for to the traditional limitations in post-exilic Judaism was added a tendency to separate woman from social life outside the home in order to "protect her morals." This was a disabling protection which put women on the same footing as those with no power of decision—children and slaves.

It can be seen, however, that women give a special welcome to the message of salvation, not only because of Jesus' open and revolutionary attitude toward them but also because of their own persistence in approaching the Master.

Let us give some examples:

- The "known sinner" who burst into the house of Simon—a Pharisee, no less—praises and anoints Jesus. This woman, who certainly had touched rock bottom socially, recognizes Jesus Christ as the Lord not only on account of those with whom he eats but on her own account as a dispossessed woman; and that is why she is ready to receive his gracious forgiveness and be open to it. She was in quest of salvation.
- Another interesting example is that of the widow who contributes her offering: a real symbol in the hands of woman, and a poor one, amid the ostentation of the rich. Let us not forget Jesus' judgment on the scribes who "devour widows' houses." This

woman honors the act of giving with her two tiny coins, snatched from her means of support.

- Mary, the sister of Martha, also responds to Christ in an unconventional way reflecting a new and deep understanding of her relationship to Christ as a woman. She leaves her "natural" activities which are socially approved and discovers that she can sit down and listen and learn. Not only does she accept Jesus as the Master, but she relativizes her concern for the set patterns of her daily life. Mary recognizes a special time and presence when Jesus is visiting.

In these examples, we find women giving up their passive attitude and asserting themselves in society, recognizing the new opening created by a new attitude of Christ which establishes confidence and makes reconciliation possible. Their actions do not amount to a change on a community level, and so do not produce similar attitudes in other women, but they join the community around Christ and are "fellow workers"; though none of them has the status of disciple or apostle. We have to evaluate this in the socio-cultural context of the age and not miss the valuable features in these attitudes.

The Church Reproduces Oppressive Structures: Marginalization of Women

THE CHURCH IN CRISIS

It is not necessary here to review the history of the Church in order to see how the situation of women has progressed or regressed from the time of Christ—partly because that would go beyond the purpose of this essay but primarily because we women want to see our present situation in the light of the message of Christ. This does not mean that we have to lose the historical perspective, which will still be there, but rather that the other approach should have its proper place.

Gustavo Gutiérrez says:

> The Latin American church is in crisis. Some may try to tone down this fact or offer various interpretations of it, but that does not change the essential fact. The reality is clear enough

> and it cannot be hidden away or talked out of existence. We must face up to it boldly if we do not want to live in an imaginary world.[9]

I believe that most women, and especially those of us with a commitment and attachment to the Church and to Latin America either through our ministry or just by our faith, would say "Amen" to this statement. If we understand crisis as a time of judgment, then the time has come for our life as the Church to be radically confronted by the Word of God and by Latin American history; and perhaps the time has come when the Church cannot ride out the crisis on the basis of its doctrine or its power. I believe that this is a highly creative moment and one of profound hope, because the questions addressed to the Church, and coming from the Church itself, are an expression of other questionings and profound crises which Latin America is experiencing and which have become part and parcel of the great historical project of our liberation. It is a project in which there is a reversal of situations: Those who have been silenced are making themselves loudly heard, structures are tottering, signs of life are being discovered in the midst of a tremendous program of death. For all these reasons, we women, together with those others who are oppressed in Latin America, feel that this crisis is our great opportunity. But with unqualified realism we also must say that it is our way of the Cross on which there may for a long time be victims called upon to pay a price with their lives and afflictions and all kinds of suffering.

Will the Church be prepared for the Cross? What will be its defenses? What dangers will it be able to withstand? And with what results? Shall we in the end begin to give shape to a church which is truly Latin American in its visible appearance in the life and struggles of our peoples?

I believe that Dr. Julio Barreiro rightly places the Church in the midst of the Latin American situation in the following analysis:

> . . . the urgency of the changes Latin America has been undergoing in this last quarter of the twentieth century, is an opportunity to renew the Church, which finally must abandon its colonial or neocolonialist structures; modify the requirements of its traditions and liturgies which are foreign to the

everyday life of its members; submit to fresh examination the practical value of its structures and the true mission of its programs; listen better to *the voice of the people, and make it more forcefully heard.*[10]

We can add value to this analysis "from within"—which I think is valid and which I would like to have its place among the preoccupations of many of our churches. We can set it against the analysis and the questions raised "from the outside" emanating from non-Christian groups of intellectuals and from the wisdom of the people—that very people which has knocked at the doors of our churches and has obtained a little bit of bread or an invitation to enter an unfamiliar and systematized world where it has not felt any desire to remain.

The Churches' Internal Debt to Latin America

Latin America is burdened with an enormous foreign debt which, as a young Argentine has said, "swallows up our efforts" . . . "the debt is claiming the lives of our children, old folk, and workers."[11] This debt is the diabolical expression of an international economic order which has devised a program of robbery, exploitation, and death for Latin America. It is a debt which is paid by the poorest, by the mere fact that they have been born at this time and place. It is increasingly creating a deep gap between the oppressed and the oppressors—two groups which are becoming irreconcilable within this system.

We, the churches in Latin America, have an enormous internal debt—*paradoxically*—to the same sectors of society. What are the signs of this debt? Let us list those we think the most important:

In the first place there is the *institutionalization of the historical Churches,* which reproduce the values, structures, theology, options, and problems of the "mother," "missionary" churches which irrupted into Latin America from the developed world at various junctures in the conquest and colonization of Latin America (Spanish and English conquests and North American colonialism). These churches identified themselves with the aims of their countries and worked through preaching and education, "shaping" the new model of humanity and society. What is more, they legitimized the new system, degrading the displaced or destroyed classes so that the new culturalization and economic, political, and social order could be established.

Consequently some thirty years ago the social, economic, and political models of Latin America began to be called in question on the basis of the people's struggles. While the churches had kept themselves comfortably established in their "evangelizing" mission without any questioning from the Gospels, a widespread situation of injustice, which began at the very time the first *conquistadores* disembarked, grew up. What is more, they silenced their prophets and their protesters so that they could keep intact their increasing dependence on the centers of power.

What was the situation of the poor in this church scenario?

- Receivers of charity.

> . . . charity, on the one hand, consists in working technically for the development of the bourgeois world and, on the other hand, in helping the underdeveloped countries to assimilate to effect better the values and principles of bourgeois society and make it their own. In other words, charity would plainly only be self-love, since the aid is primarily a contribution to those who distribute it! Even many grants for students are not intended to prepare the way for future openings.[12]

- Those who are passed over and silenced.

From the time when—just a few decades ago—the decisions relating to the life and work of our churches were made by the missionary churches (which still happens in the churches which were not autonomous), on into the new stage in which the organization has been put in the hands of lay and ordained people steeped in the theology and ideology of the central churches, we have seen that the poor have only had the little leeway allowed to them by the structures in force. Women, Indians, young people, and blacks also share in this situation. All the marginalized groups have traditionally had little or no influence on decisions and even less possibility of effecting change.

As to the specific situation of women, after five hundred years of Spanish colonization (the coming of Roman Catholicism) and a hundred and fifty years of Protestant presence in a continent with a female population numerically superior to the male, we still see that:

- the churches continue to choose their leaders, with some exceptions, from the educated, predominantly white and male, middle classes.
- There are very few instances indeed of women chair-persons or bishops although there is an increasingly large number of ordained women.
- On the local congregational level, women are being kept at the work of teaching or the diaconate without being able to participate to any great extent in the Church's theological and political discussions and without their standpoint being taken into account as a factor in opinion.
- Within our churches, there is rejection on a further level, of prostitutes, unmarried mothers, homosexual women and, in many churches, woman revolutionaries and intellectuals or simply women who are restless politically.

In the second place, there is a *conspiratorial silence*. The Western and Christian world, which tries to be the exponent and defender of true democracy in the world, has produced, as a correlate of its political and economic system, a lethal ideological tool: the doctrine of national security.

The practical expression of this is militarism, through which the moderately promising process experienced in Latin America in the 'sixties has been successfully choked off and distorted. In various sister countries, new models of a nascent socialism were emerging and have already become a reality in Cuba.

To these projects, which were encouraging hope for an end to the robbery and sacrifices to which we have been subjected by North American imperialism, the enemy responded by meticulously organizing a system of repression under the banner of "the struggle against communism." The purpose of this was to continue the exploitation of Latin America in its new form of internalizing capital and labor and ensuring peaceful ways of taking the spoils.

To achieve this plan, it was necessary:

- to pervert the state and change it into the hostile repressor of the people;
- to turn the armed forces into highly technological, highly-tuned death machines;
- to win over the dominant Creole classes by turning them into agents who are traitors to their own people;
- to silence every voice; to imprison, torture, and kill hundreds of thousands of our Latin American brothers and sisters, especially peasants, workers, students, i.e., the poor.

I have called this part *conspiratorial silence*. Although from the Christian churches there has arisen a cry of grief, rage, and resistance to these violations, and although we can number many Christians among the martyrs, exiles, and victims of torture, the Latin American churches, both Catholic and Protestant, cannot hide either that they have been shamefully silent at the hierarchical institutional level, unable to sever their ties of economic, ideological, and theological dependence on the centers of power in various countries of Latin America. Unquestionably, sectors of the Church have cooperated in repression and torture. To this we must add the pseudo-ecclesiastical phenomena, sects which up and down our continent proclaim themselves churches of Christ and operate as an alienating factor, as the effective voice of imperialistic purposes.

Thirdly, *the inability to read historically the signs of our times* is another of our debts as churches to Latin America. With eyes focused on the centers of power of the developed world, we have neglected incarnation in our own situation. We have not allowed ourselves to change in our theology or our structures. Thus it is that we continue to be centers of wealth in the midst of poverty—wealth which manifests itself in buildings, churches, vastly extravagant programs of education and human development, and huge commercial organizations which are a scandal in the light of the economic situation of our people.

One sign of great hope in this whole scene is represented by base Christian communities coming into being in various countries of our continent and by the revolution which the theology of liberation has provoked in Christian thought and action. These two phenomena arise out of a new awareness of the Latin American situation among militant priests and lay people committed to achieving a new presence for the Church in the world of the oppressed.

These are the most serious and audacious efforts to balance our internal debt as a church toward the people. We have not succeeded yet in freeing ourselves from our colonialist ties, nor have we faced with unwavering conviction our responsibility to proclaim a liberating Gospel. But it has been possible to do something toward radically sounding out the crisis as the conflict with traditional theology and structures of the churches has been launched. As I have already said, the crisis is of value in itself only as a means of triggering new processes by which to listen in particular to women, with all that we have to contribute to the New People of God, a people of liberation for Latin America.

Conclusion

The Historical Power of Latin American Women As Part of the People of God

I believe that the first step toward an accurate assessment of what we can achieve as women in the continent is to *become aware* of our *actual situation* among the oppressed of society. I underline this because there are still very few of us women who are equipped to carry out a scientific analysis of the Latin American situation, and among these few there are even fewer who can exercise any influence in the decision-making centers; and that is true for the whole of society and for the Church in particular.

The starting point for this growth in awareness must be to reinterpret our own history, in which the subjugation of women had its own typically brutal features: the exploitation, sexually and at work, of native women, which was prevalent at the time of the conquest, has manifested itself up to the present in ill-concealed, sophisticated ways, but ways which are consistent with the same premise: that woman is inferior to man and must be subjected to his will.

It is of basic importance to strip this situation of its *false fronts:* woman as queen in the home; woman in her beauty; woman with her intuition and her sensitivity, to the detriment of her intellectual capacity; woman as holy and as a sacrifice; woman as the co-worker of man.

It is very important to put a proper value on those situations in which woman has shown her power and conviction in the liberating struggle with men, and to support and publicize these situations: women as protesters; women who engage in the political struggle; women who think and analyze and try to gain a hearing; women as an indispensable work force.

To gain this new awareness will give us the raw material for working out strategic proposals for action, and will make it possible for us to become involved in the project of liberation of our peoples, as individuals actively defending those rights which belong to our own sex.

I consider that there are three fundamental themes which woman must develop on the basis of her commitment to society and to the Gospel:

- *Defense of life*

  Life is Latin America's sole capital for the struggle against oppression and the defense of the wealth of our land. Defense of our motherhood, which is under attack, runs through the struggle against the "system of death" which makes decisions about huge masses of human beings who are anonymous and defenseless.

  Motherhood becomes a communal and political function. It totally transcends the limits of the small family, or the household, to appeal earnestly in the streets for the right to live when confronted with impoverishment, repression, and assassination.
- *Defense of Dignity*

  The wholesale violation of human rights which we are experiencing in Latin America calls for us, as women, to reject and denounce all those situations in which human beings are reduced to "chattel," and their values, convictions, and decisions are being constantly and violently interfered with.

  This struggle becomes "subversive" in the effort to counter cultural penetration, the consumer society, sexism, and individualism as expressions of a system of life based on the accumulation of power and capital in the interests of a small group and to the detriment of the poor majorities. This system engenders antagonisms and enmities, class division, the destruction of the powers of the people, and the silencing of the aspirations of the oppressed.

The defense of human dignity has again become a public, open struggle. It is a defense with a public platform and it must be united with other efforts made on a world-wide basis. It is a defense which results in concrete changes of economic, social, and political structures which may make possible a wholesale revision of the established order.

- *Defense of one's "womanhood"*

Undoubtedly, the traditional roles need to be revised thoroughly, as they give rise to a social order in which men are privileged in every walk of life, and legalize it. This is not "natural," as many women still believe, nor is it the product of circumstance. It can, on the contrary, be changed, and this will happen if we women really make up our minds to do so.

The greatest reason for raising the question of equal rights and status for men and women lies in acknowledging not only the difference between the sexes but also of their unavoidable and necessary unity for procreation and for the maintenance of life. The fulfillment of this common destiny, which begins with the choice of one's partner, has become for us something passive, in which we have to hope for the favor of being chosen by the man—for whom traditionally we have to reserve the whole gift of our untouched, undefiled bodies, unconditionally handing over our lives to him.

To be a woman was ultimately to be the object of the man's choice, or else to remain unattached. To change this situation is essentially to claim recognition as persons, as beings in charge of our own personal and social history, to choose in full freedom the use of our potentialities, and to recognize in the other party someone who can take the initiative, a free person like ourselves. I believe that in this way it is possible to recreate in unusually creative and humanizing ways all the relations between men and women as they are expressed in the following terms: husband and wife; mother and son; comrades at work; comrades in the struggles of liberation.

Our Responsibility As Part of the People of God

From the standpoint of faith, we feel that we are part of the People of God, of that people called to freedom and salvation—the

People of God, is at the same time the mystery of the presence of the risen Christ and the sociological expression of human activity at a particular juncture in history. We are part of that people and, as such, we are on the move, both in the historical process and transcendentally, toward a *kairos* that has been proclaimed: the time of the Kingdom which in part we know and toward which we are in part looking forward. As the People of God, we feel we are called to move forward toward the fulfillment of a divine covenant of salvation for all humanity and also to unite in a visible community which is the sign of the final fulfillment, and into which all those who accept the requirements of the covenant with God must be brought. As women, we feel our scope for movement reduced and constricted by the manifestations of human sin which, turning its back on God, has created structures of domination by some people over others. Our responsibility then is dual. We must go forward with the people in its struggle for liberation and for salvation which must be expressed in signs of life, love, and solidarity. But at the same time, we must reaffirm from God's revelation our own liberation as "created in the image and likeness (of God)," called to an equal status with men and united in the community of all who believe in Christ, as sensitive and thinking women who have received the message of salvation and can effectively proclaim that message to all humanity.

Taking on this dual responsibility will contribute to hastening the downfall of the obsolete structures which imprison the power of the Gospel and the potentialities of the People of God in a false interpretation of what it means for us to be the Church; and at the same time it will provide an opportunity for the emergence of new expressions of the Church which are more faithful to the demands of the Gospel.

7

The Prophetic Ministry of Women in the Hebrew Bible

Tereza Cavalcanti

The reconsideration of prophetic ministry in recent years has awakened considerable interest, particularly in those who live with the present-day problems of the Church in Latin America. This may be due to the fact that critical accountability is an ongoing and unavoidable necessity in a society in which structural contrasts and injustice appeal to Christian conscience. In crises such as these, one sees new examples of communal commitment, as well as creative practices, which are developed by the poor in their privation and oppression, tying their faith to historical reality. A significant aspect of this popular Christian movement which has spread throughout Latin America is the presence and activity of women committed to the life and liberation of the poor. We will focus on these two themes: prophetic ministry and the role of women.

Our main objective is to deal with both of these themes as they occur in the Hebrew Bible. What prophetic ministry did women have among the people of Israel? What differences might there have

---

Translated from Spanish by Jeltje Aukema

been between the prophetic roles of women and men? Does the prophetic role of women have anything in common with Jesus' prophetic ministry? How might this help Christian communities today, especially those communities in Latin America and in the third world?

These are our questions. Before we search for answers we will discuss methodological considerations.

Methodology

As is obvious from the description of our objectives, these reflections do not pretend to be neutral. Far from it. We are trying to be sensitive to the questions that are welling up in a Church whose place among the poor demands a faithful, and at the same time renewed, rereading of the scriptures. We are also conscious of the need for exegetical and biblical theological support for our thesis. Thus, we are confronted with a number of limitations and difficulties which must be kept in mind as we go along.

Since the biblical texts were written in the context of a patriarchal society, materials related to our theme are few and far between. This limitation has been reinforced by the fact that women have for so long been considered inferior to men, both in the Church and in society. Theological reflection has mirrored this reality, both in what is spoken, and what remains unsaid.

We realize that with this lack of information we run the risk of forcing an interpretation on the biblical texts in light of a predetermined objective. To what extent is it legitimate to reread the Bible from the perspective of women's more highly-valued status today, given the generally second-class status which women occupy in the Hebrew Bible?

We raise questions about methodology because of the above mentioned concerns. The circumstances point to a methodological choice which can address both exegetical and theological concerns—in relationship to the practice of the Church.

In order to deal with this subject from women's perspective, on the exegetical as well as hermeneutical level, the aforementioned limits and objectives point to the inadequacy of using only historical-critical methodology. Limiting ourselves to this method would mean that we would never address our concerns. This methodology must be supplemented, and in some cases replaced with structural analysis.[1] This method allows us to relativize the written text, without depreciating it entirely. Sometimes this will serve as the point of departure; other times the point of departure will be what has been omitted from the text, that is, the silence of the text. Having identified our methodology, we can say that within a text that is markedly patriarchal, where favoritism of men prevails to the detriment of women, it is perfectly understandable that these texts would contain many more references to men's prophetic ministry than to women's. As unlikely as it may seem in such a patriarchal context, Israel did have women prophets. This bias makes any mention of women even more significant. The reason for our methodological choice is that, while the biblical texts identify several women prophets (Deborah, Hulda, Miriam), they tell us little or nothing about what they did. Moreover, this cultural discrimination means that those without an indepth knowledge of the scriptures may completely miss the accounts of women prophets since they are hidden among accounts of their better-known male counterparts. While it may seem strange to speak of women prophets, the Bible does refer to them; this means that we are obligated to do so as well.

We want to deal with the texts, on a theological level as they relate to the practice of the Church, in a way that goes beyond simple literal interpretation. Thus, in the space which is opened and at the same time circumscribed by "hermeneutical reason,"[2] there is an attempt to grasp the "spiritual sense" of the communities' experience. Far from being an abstraction or disembodied purism, the spiritual sense is related to what Carlos Mesters calls the Bible's "sense-for-us." This means "the sense that God reveals to us by his Spirit, through the ancient biblical texts."[3] In fact, there is no rupture but continuity between what was revealed to the people of God in the past and the breath of the Spirit that accompanies the reading of the Bible within faith communities today.[4] From this perspective, we will reread the explicit and implicit texts from the Hebrew Bible referring to the prophetic ministry of women.

In consideration of the specific nature of our subject material, we have decided to forego general descriptions of the prophetic ministry, as well as of the social and legal situation of women during this period. This information is fairly well known and it can be found in other studies. Pressing questions from the past as well as from the present lead us directly to a commentary on the texts.

Women's Prophetic Ministry

Two types of biblical texts lend themselves to a study of the prophetic ministry of women: those which explicitly mention women prophets and those which describe women acting prophetically, in the broad sense of the word.

Wise Women and Prophets

In spite of rules that favor men while socially and culturally discriminating against women, there are some biblical texts which draw attention to wise and courageous women for responding to a particular call.[5] We are pleased to note explicit references in the Hebrew Bible to Hulda (2 Kings 22:14), Deborah (Judg. 4:4ff), Miriam (Exod. 15:20), and the nameless woman in Isaiah (8:3).

Hulda was a temple prophet. According to the text, she is consulted by five people including Hilkiah the priest. She prophesied in favor of the true God and against man-made idols which are useless and illusory.

Deborah is a prophet and one of the leaders of the people during the time of the judges. The narrative shows that Deborah came into her position of leadership gradually. When first introduced, she is sitting under a palm tree in the highlands of Ephraim between Ramah and Bethel. Here she waited for Israelites who passed through this area; she was known for settling disputes. In verse 6, Deborah calls Barak to her to tell him that God has ordered him to mobilize the troops for war. Verse 8 includes a response from Barak, surprising given the patriarchal context:

> Barak answered her, "If you come with me, I will go; if you will not come, I will not go, for I do not know how to choose the day when the angel of Yahweh will grant me success" (Judg. 4:8).

Finally, in chapter 5:12, we hear a persistent call: "Wake up!" Awake from what, for what? In the context of the previous account, a response is not necessary; the response is implicit. "Awake, awake, Deborah! Awake, awake, declaim a song!" The cry for Deborah can be taken as an invitation to women to wake up and take up their task in the history of the salvation of their people.

Miriam, the sister of Aaron and Moses (Exod. 15:20), went into the streets with a tambourine, dancing and praising God for their new freedom. The women followed her with their tambourines also singing the song of Miriam and Moses.

Little is known about the woman prophet in Isaiah except that Isaiah, who was a great prophet of justice, considered her a prophet (8:3). She bore him a child whose symbolic name is related to the prophetic mission. This anonymity is characteristic of many women who assumed a prophetic role and wisely influenced and guided the leaders of their people.

We can see a gradual broadening of prophetic ministry in the Hebrew Bible (cf. Judges 1–2). This tendency coincides with today's idea of the prophetic role, whether it be individual or collective, particularly among oppressed peoples. This is the case in the third world. We understand women's biblical prophetic role in this wider sense of the word; this understanding can also be applied to the Latin American context today.

Even though they were not called prophets, the prophetic work of women like Judith, Esther, Ruth, Tamar, Anna, and others had great impact on the social, political, and religious life of their people. Some of these elements will be identified in a study of pertinent texts.

Claiming Their Rights: "Awake!"

The prophetic ministry of women in the Hebrew Bible is somewhat different from that of men in that it consists more of *exhortation* than of *denunciation*. Women speak out in order to encourage the people not to give up but to defend themselves and engage themselves in struggle. That is what the cry for Deborah, "Awake!" is all about (Judg. 5:12). It also means awakening the conscience of those who are violating the rights of the powerless.

Women in these stories seem to be constantly reclaiming their few and oft-violated rights. Thus, we see Tamar (who appears, however briefly, in the genealogy in Matthew) demanding that her father-in-law, Judah, fulfill the levirate code and the right to descendants. It was a question of life and future survival for her. In response to her brave appeal, Judah finally admits: "She is in the right, rather than I" (Gen. 38:26).

In the same way, and with the approval of her mother-in-law, Naomi, Ruth used her rights as a widow and a foreigner to glean grain in the fields (Ruth 2:2ff.). Then, in a discreet and courageous way, Ruth let Boaz know that he was neglecting his duties toward her as a relative (3:1–9). In a sketchy way, the book of Ruth shows how two women without recourse or power—which in any case was not their goal—encouraged a man to fulfill his duties to them. They convinced Boaz that his kind words were not enough:

> "May Yahweh reward you for what you have done! May rich recompense be made to you by Yahweh, the God of Israel, to whom you have come to find shelter beneath his wings" (Ruth 2:12).

Boaz needed to put his praise into action.[6] The seemingly inconsequential acts of these two women had revolutionary repercussions in respect to family, sustenance, and descendants because they pointed out the importance of a contract between two parties. Israel could not forget the Law, given by God and guaranteed by the Covenant. And finally, if Ruth and Naomi had not insisted that Boaz fulfill the law, David would never have been born.[7]

Esther's circumstances are different. While living under the domination of the Persians, the Jewish people face annihilation in a troubling decree:

> . . . letters were sent by runners to every province of the realm ordering the destruction, slaughter and annihilation of all Jews, young and old, women and children, on the one day . . . (Esther 3:13)

Queen Esther was a Jew. When her uncle Mordecai warned her of the decree, she took on the difficult task of the liberation of her people. Civil disobedience was the Jewish people's only recourse in a situation like this. They often used this method during their exiles in foreign lands.[8] Using the cunning available to her as a woman and as a queen, Esther risks everything and wins her case.

The oppressed (Mordecai) is given the oppressor's (Haman) position and the decree is rescinded (8:11–12).

Thus, in different texts of the Hebrew Bible we see women reminding men of the traditions of the people, and demanding that the law be fulfilled and the rights of the weakest respected. Isn't this prophetic ministry? We know that men prophets fought for this same cause; they were protagonists of justice. The difference between their ministries is that the men prophets threatened and warned of severe punishments while the women prophets only called people to remember the faith and to act decisively and concretely in defense of the people or for those who suffered injustice. How can we explain that men from such a patriarchal society listened to women and did not scorn their message? From whence came the power and the authority of these women prophets?

Authority, Leadership, and Wisdom

It is significant that the Hebrew Bible refers to many women who took on the responsibilities of prophet and that there was at least one woman judge (Deborah). Yet, there is no mention whatsoever of any women serving as priest or levite nor of their taking on military responsibilities. Esther's influence was related to her position as wife of the king, and it could be revoked at any time. Deborah and Judith both played the same sort of role in regard to the soldiers: they both cleared the way so that the soldiers could, through armed combat, defend their threatened people.

What kind of power did these women have? In the Hebrew Bible they did not seem to be part of institutionalized power, nor a part of the armed forces. What then, was the basis for their authority?

It is interesting to see how the texts praise the wise woman and how this wisdom becomes a form of feminine leadership. The courageous and wise, even bold, display of this leadership usually takes place in times of grave crisis when a lack of male leadership threatens the people's survival.

Judith appears in a situation like this to act decisively to save her people (Jth. 8:1ff.). We see in her a combination of wisdom and strong leadership, which she uses skillfully to oppose a decision made by the city fathers which threatened the people's survival. Judith made them aware of the danger of their decision so that they could act wisely. She used words similar to those found in the book of Wisdom (Wis. 9:13; Jth. 8:14). Judith is praised for her upright life, which reinforced her prophetic leadership.

Ruth, too, is praised for her upright and virtuous life. It provided the community with a quiet but firm kind of leadership. The words of Boaz attest to the respect she received: ". . . for the people of Bethlehem all know your worth" (Ruth 3:11b).

In the story of Deborah, the prophetic ministry and the office of judge is combined in the same person:

> At this time Deborah was judge in Israel, a prophetess, the wife of Lappidoth. She used to sit under Deborah's Palm between Ramah and Bethel in the highlands of Ephraim, and the Israelites would come to her to have their disputes decided (Judg. 4:4–5).

Thus, we see that wisdom is a common factor for both prophets and judges. Wisdom has to do with one's desire for justice and with a sensitive reading of the signs of the times. These are also qualities of the prophets. Wisdom is associated with life experience, with the slow learning about life that comes only with age and time. The wise know the importance of historical patience. They know how to wait for the proper moment and they recognize the right opportunity for each gesture (Ecclus. 3:1–8). This is why Judith would not "test" God's intervention. She told the elders of the town to plead to God for help and to "wait patiently for him to save" (Jth. 8:17).

Linked to their wisdom in "giving time time," there is another characteristic of women prophets in the Bible, which is their capacity to resist.

Symbol of the People's Resistance

Israel often faced crises; usually these crises meant that Israel faced extinction. The official leaders could not always help in such situations. When this was the case, the leadership vacuum was often filled by women who came forward on their own initiative, or in response to an explicit call. The women who occupied these positions of leadership felt called to protect the life of their people, and to prevent the dissolution of the promise and covenant with God.

Deborah appeared at a time when the people were discouraged and weak:

> ''Dead, dead were Israel's villages
> until you rose up, O Deborah,
> you rose up, a mother in Israel'' (Judg. 5:7).

This song was written a little after the events it praises (about 1125 B.C.). It may be one of the oldest biblical texts and one of the few written by women.[9]

The book of Ruth was written at the time of the Israelites' return from slavery, when Esdras ordered all foreign women expelled from the country. It is a story of popular resistance. The important bits of information are not explicit, but symbolic. They are revealed through the names of the characters, gestures, and ironical allusions (Ruth, the protagonist of the story, is a widow and a foreigner).[10] Ruth and Naomi symbolize the inflexible resistance of those who will neither forget their rights nor let others forget them.

Judith, as was noted above, shows the elders of the town that resistance need not be passive, and that faith does not change with despair (Jth. 8). Imagine the effect this book had! It was written at the height of oppression, during the period of Greek domination and the reaction of the Maccabees. Judith's genealogy is the longest of any woman in the Bible (16 names!). She symbolizes an end to the panic and abandonment of the struggle, the negation—by a woman!—of the capitulation on the part of male leadership. Further on we will see where Judith got her extraordinary strength.[11]

There is a similar display of wisdom and leadership in 2 Samuel 20:16–22. Here, a woman, whose name is not recorded, saves a city from being destroyed.

In Esther's case, the resistance movement, prompted by the threat of the extinction of her people, comes about through a series of initiatives, exchange of messages, and finally a strategy for the restoration of their threatened rights.

When focussing on the history of prophetic feminine resistance, we cannot overlook the mother of the Maccabees, whose name is also omitted, despite the importance of her contribution. She emerged in an apocalyptic context, caused by the extreme oppression of her people.

> . . . [She] is no longer an average woman. She was turned into an "image," that is, she became the symbol of a people who resists, who recall their history and work out a counter-ideology which supports the people in their resistance and struggle. She "produced" a new mystique of life at a time when *death* reigned. . . . It is not simply a coincidence that, at this same time, faith in the resurrection became popular. And, in the book in question, it is a woman who, faced with a terribly violent situation, worked out this faith.[12]

The fact that the mother of the Maccabees remains anonymous, as do many other women, makes us think about their place among the people. Resistance struggles are undoubtedly collective struggles.

Solidarity with the People in the Option for Life

Ruth did not abandon her mother-in-law Naomi even though it meant denying herself a future, which at that time meant descendants. One of the most impressive lines in the story is Ruth's pledge of allegiance to Naomi after having been offered the chance to go back to her people and a future. In solidarity with Naomi and her people, Ruth said:

> "Do not press me to leave you and to turn back from your company, for
>
> > "wherever you go, I will go,
> > wherever you live, I will live.
> > Your people shall be my people,
> > and your God, my God.
> > Wherever you die, I will die
> > and there I will be buried. . . . " (Ruth 1:16ff)[13]

In Esther, chapter 4, we see a woman faced with a dramatic and conflictive situation in which she can opt for solidarity with her people, at the risk of her life, or play it safe. She could have kept quiet and allowed her people to be massacred. Courageously, she opts for life and solidarity with her people.

Deborah, on the other hand, is the one who calls the dispersed tribes of Israel together. Seeing that the warriors have responded to her call, she breaks out in a song:

> "My heart beats fast for Israel's chieftains,
> with those of the people who stood forth boldly.
> For this, bless Yahweh!" (Judg. 5:9)

Solidarity in the struggle, like the people's voluntary participation, is reinforced by God's intervention through natural elements: even the stars and the waters (Judg. 5:20–21) participate in the struggle.

Though the struggles of collective resistance in Deborah, Judith, and Miriam (Exod. 15:20) reach almost "epic" proportions, in other contexts, solidarity assumes less spectacular forms. For example, when individuals in a "complicit" way align themselves against the oppressor. Sometimes, this kind of underground alliance includes even members of neighboring peoples or tribes who join with the Israelites out of sensitivity to injustice. This was the case with Jael (Judg. 4:17), the Egyptian midwives (Exod. 1:15–21), Rahab (Josh. 2), and Ruth. It is interesting to note that God, too, enters into this "complicity" on behalf of the oppressed. The story of the slave Hagar is a particularly vivid account of such complicity on God's part (Gen. 16:11; 21:17–20).

The oppressed can silently resist by organizing themselves; this way it is possible to bring together a whole list of experiences of oppression and injustice, and communicate them to the community. Milton Schwantes' study of the prophet Amos reveals a list of crimes committed against the poor on numerous occasions:

> . . . because they have sold the virtuous man for silver and the poor man for a pair of sandals, because they trample on the heads of ordinary people and push the poor out of their path, because father and son have both resorted to the same girl, profaning my holy name, because they stretch themselves out by side of every altar on clothes acquired as pledges,

> and drink the wine of the people they have fined in the house of their god . . . (Amos 2:6b–8).

Schwantes points out

> . . . the organizational significance inherent in this list. When all is said and done this presupposes that this experience of suffering by some was communicated to others. Pain is shared in groups. . . . We can say that the denunciation of verses 6b–8 reflects a collective experience of oppression. For this reason, the existence of a list of grievances presupposes the existence of an organization of those who suffer and work under injustice.[14]

It is not difficult to imagine what role women played in this organization, particularly in the passing on of messages. Reading between the lines, this participation is seen in Deborah's song where she shows how well informed she is about what was happening among the tribes of Israel. The same can be said of Ruth and Naomi, Esther, Judith, and Tamar.

The communal dimension is essential for women's prophetic ministry. If women surface as leaders only when there is a leadership crisis, it is not because they do not normally have the ability to do so. Rather, it is because women are *identified with the whole of the people,* whose traditions they preserve and pass on from generation to generation.[15] Another reason is that where there are no people to support them and to whom they are accountable, there are no leaders. If these leaders don't come through, the people must stand firm and weather the crisis. In this unbroken succession in which life is recreated and reinvented in order to find new ways to overcome death, the prophetic presence of women reveals their tenacity to fight to the end for that which they consider God's will.

Faith in the God of the Oppressed Who Makes a Covenant with the People

The authority of the women prophets also comes from their faith in the God of the oppressed.

"Your strength does not lie in numbers,
nor your might in violent men;
since you are the God of the humble,
the help of the oppressed,
the support of the weak,
the refuge of the forsaken,
the savior of the despairing" (Jth. 9:11).

Here we find a faith woven over years of resistance, a faith that is weather-beaten, yet still reborn in suffering and joy. Why does this kind of faith appeal to people? Because, in recovering the people's faith in God, the people's faith in themselves as the people of God is recovered, along with their hope for liberation in the future.[16] An important aspect of prophetic ministry in Israel, particularly as this role is exercised by women, is the conviction that rights of the poor are God-given rights.

> In the Bible, this sense of the people's faith can inspire a spiritual current characterized by their peculiar way of placing their faith in God. In the tradition of the Church, under certain circumstances, this faith may seem unusual or shocking. Today we rediscover its deep roots in the revelation process. We find ourselves better able to grasp God's profundity which is the spirituality of the people as it has survived over the generations.[17]

Hannah's song (I Samuel 2:1–10), which might be the first edition of Mary's Magnificat, demands that God have a preference for the poor:

He raises the poor from the dust,
  he lifts the needy from the dunghill
to give them a place with princes,
  and to assign them a seat of honor;
for to Yahweh the props of the earth belong,
  on these he has poised the world (I Sam. 2:8).

The book of Ruth, too, reflects this conviction that God acts alongside the humble and the scorned. The law is seen as protecting the weak and those who cannot fight for their rights. The law redeems, and that which redeems turns out to be the relationship of Yahweh with Yahweh's people.

> What Boaz did for Ruth portrays what God does for God's people. Boaz spread his coat over Ruth (Ruth 3:9), which reminds us of God spreading his coat over his people, his bride (Ezek. 16:8). In Deutero-Isaiah, the name *Goel* (redeemer, defender) frequently refers to God.[18]

Nevertheless, faith in the God of the poor is accompanied by a sense of responsibility for the covenant. From this sense of responsibility comes a strong prophetic accent on faithfulness to that covenant. Women watch over the people's faithfulness in order to remind the people to live such that the promises of God may find the way prepared for their fulfillment. God does not need to be reminded of God's promises; the people of God must make room for the realization of these promises. The contractual relationship between God and Israel is viable only when those who suffer injustice are attended to. The nation's honor is at stake in honoring those without legal recourse.[19]

Women remind the people of their responsibilities several different times in the Hebrew Bible. Through their activity, faith in the true and only God is set in opposition to faith in pagan idols. Their objective is to make the people of the covenant remember; they accomplish this by reminding them of their past, that is, by referring to historical memory. Thus, we see Judith reminding the people of what the Lord did for them during the time of the patriarchs (Jth. 8:18, 25–27). We also have Hulda warning king Josiah about keeping the law (2 Kings 22:14).

The relationship of strong, persistent faith in the God of the covenant is expressed in peculiar ways in the prophetic ministry of women: jubilant hymns, or cries of lamentation. We will comment on the latter.

Cries of Lamentation

Living as they did under foreign rule and an oppressive regime, in poverty and danger, the people of Israel knew what it was to have their strength choked off and their ability to resist falter. In these times of crisis, in which hope seemed to vanish, their last recourse was to cry to Yahweh. From their experience in Egypt, the people of Israel knew how to cry to God, and they knew that their cries were not in vain.[20]

Four steps mark the events of the book of Judges:

- The people do something that is not pleasing to God.
- Yahweh lets the people of God fall into the hands of the enemy.
- Israel cries to God.
- Yahweh hears their cries and sends a liberator.

The cry is not just a request for help; it is also a public expression of the people's pain, an externalization of the pain of the whole nation.

In Esther, for example, the lament was not directed at God but it was meant to raise consciousness, and provoke a response from the people.[21] The Jews mourned, fasted, wept, wailed, and many put on sackcloth and ashes (Esther 4:1–3). In preparation for risking her life by going before the king, Esther fasted and asked the people to fast with her.

Judith associated fasting with prayer, and the salvation of Israel with the preservation of the Temple. She showed that Israel's problems are God's problems; that was why Israel should have faith in the God of their forefathers (Jth. 8:21–24). Judith's prayer is one of the most beautiful prayers in the Bible (Jth. 9). The introduction affirms the relationship between the human cry and the divine response:

> Judith threw herself face to the ground, scattered ashes on her head, uncovered the sackcloth she was wearing and cried loudly to the Lord. At the same time in Jerusalem the evening incense was being offered in the Temple of God. . . . (Jth. 9:1)

Judith was a woman who identified with the suffering of her people. She bowed down and prayed as a mediator for their salvation. Her cry went up at the same time as the evening incense was being offered to the One who is the "help of the oppressed" (9:11).

In the book of Ruth, Naomi is the one who cries:

"Do not call me Naomi, call me Mara, for Shaddai (the Powerful One) has marred me bitterly.

> "Filled full I departed,
> Yahweh brings me back empty.
> Why call me Naomi, then,
> since Yahweh has given witness against me
> and Shaddai has afflicted me?" (Ruth 1:20–21)[22]

Naomi does not express her sadness directly to God, but to the women who recognize her upon her return to Bethlehem. Even before this, when she was trying to convince her daughters-in-law to return to their homes, she said: ". . . the hand of Yahweh has been raised against me" (1:13).

The whole first chapter of Ruth seems to be a lamentation devoid of hope; it speaks of hunger, sickness, death, separation, and loneliness. The only bright spot is Ruth's decision. The text refers also to the circumstances of the people at this time. It tells the story of two women who were left alone, like the rest of Israel. Yet,

> in repeating twice that the woman was left alone (1:3–5), the book of Ruth calls our attention to the prophecies which assure that with the little that is left over, a new beginning will be made (Isa. 4:3; 6:13; 10:21; 11:16; 37:31; Esd. 9:8, 15). This passage alludes to the fact that Naomi, the image of the suffering people, is the seed of a new nation.[23]

The cry of Hagar, the servant of Sarah who was cast out into the desert, cannot be overlooked in a study of the lament. As it is told in two different traditions, Yahwist (Gen. 16:1–2, 4–14) and Elohist (Gen. 21:8–21), the story of Hagar portrays a foreign woman slave who has been rejected three times.[24] In both accounts, God listens to the desperate cry of Hagar and her son. The son's name is Ismael, which means "God listens" or "God heard." Hagar may be seen as a prophetic figure for various reasons. She is the only woman in the Hebrew Bible to experience a theophany, otherwise the exclusive privilege of the great leaders and prophets of Israel. Yet, she is chosen to witness this theophany because Yahweh heard her cry of suffering (Gen. 16:11). Furthermore, in her surprise that God would appear to a foreign slave woman, Hagar calls God "the one who sees me" (v. 13). The God who hears the cries of the people is the same one who sees the anguish of the oppressed and opens the way for a new future.

The cry of the women prophets of the Bible is in line with the cries of Israel in Egypt, and it will lead to the cry of Jesus, who, throughout his life and until the time of his death, took up the cry of the suffering and the oppressed of the world.[25]

The counterpart of this cry is the response of Yahweh to those who keep the covenant. And when the Lord responds, the cry of the people is transformed into song and hymns of praise.

Songs and Hymns

Miriam is the first woman called a prophet in the Hebrew Bible. She emerges during a time of explosive joy when Israel is freed from the domination of the Egyptians. Moses, accompanied by all the children of Israel, begins a song and Miriam, carried away by the excitement of the victory, picks up a tambourine and begins to dance (Exod. 15:20). Other women follow her with their tambourines, dancing and singing: "Sing of Yahweh: he has covered himself in glory, horse and rider he has thrown into the sea" (15:21).

Nothing more is said about Miriam's prophetic ministry. It was this moment of leadership in expressing the joy of the people before their Liberator that gave Miriam a place in Israelite history. Many since have echoed her song.

Deborah, known as the "mother of Israel" (Judg. 5:7), took up the task of encouraging the people and organizing them so that they could defend themselves. After the victory had been won, again it was Deborah who encouraged the song of praise and preserved forever the memory of the covenant of Yahweh with those who fought for freedom.

The book of Ruth begins with a mood of sad desolation and ends with the joyful song of the women gathered around Naomi (4:14–15). God is praised and Naomi is "compensated" with a new will to live and the birth of her grandson. Ruth is praised by her mother-in-law as having greater value than seven sons. The neighboring women celebrate the birth of the child and with it the rebirth of their hope. The name these women give the child has a prophetic ring to it: Obed means "servant." He is listed in the genealogy of the Messiah.

Judith, too, finishes her work of liberation with a song of gratitude (Jth. 16:1–17). The liberator God is praised along with the creator God (v. 15). The lowly are raised up along with the women, who, by using their feminine resources, destroyed the enemy's power and gave the people back their confidence. In true prophetic style, Judith's last song shows contempt for sacrifices and burnt offerings, reaffirming the fundamental importance of faith (v. 16): "Whoever fears the Lord is great forever."

We see here the firm and constant faith that is the basis of a special relationship between Israel and God. A new characteristic of this covenant relationship is freedom in fidelity.

Hannah, the mother of Samuel (1 Samuel 1:20), sings a messianic song of the hope of the poor which is later taken up by Mary in the Magnificat.[26] As a woman who suffered from not being able to bear children, Hannah identified with the hope of all those scorned and marginalized by society.

Deborah stands out with her joyful song of victory (Judg. 5). The battle is described in a lively and picturesque way. It includes Yahweh as an active figure in the struggle (v. 4) and at the same time as a spectator (v. 5). The writer does not forget to name the tribes that have responded to her call, as well as those that evaded it. Meroz, a city of the tribe of Naphtali, is cursed for not responding to the call; it is judged as having refused to serve God (v. 23). In describing Sisera's demise, the song is full of irony, particularly when it mentions Sisera's mother and the women of the court watching for him through the lattice (v. 28–30). And, while these women are portrayed as ridiculous, Jael, the heroine, is praised as being "blessed among women . . . among all women that dwell in tents . . ." (v. 24).[27] The heart of the song, however, is found in verse 12:

> "Awake, awake, Deborah!
> Awake, awake, declaim a song!
> Take heart, arise Barak,
> capture your captors, son of Abinoam!"

Freedom and Fidelity

Together, freedom and fidelity form a characteristic of the prophetic biblical ministry. Judith's boldness can be explained only by the strength of her faith. The liberator God frees people from the limitations of their faith tradition. This tradition should not be confused with unchangeable formulas of the past; it is reborn in each historical moment as a continuation of the people's memory. Hence, this attitude of faith provides the necessary security and support for the new and creative gestures enacted among the people, for example, the gestures of Tamar and Ruth.

Judith, Esther, and Ruth did not hesitate to use their feminine charms and resources in defense of their people's cause. This can be understood only as an expression of their freedom and conviction: They were convinced that God was on their side. When we talk of freedom, we are referring to the freedom that is linked to faith in a God who is faithful to the people of God: God's faithfulness is partial. The God of the Bible takes the side of the marginalized, putting honor on the line in defense of the oppressed. God's partiality applies even to foreign women (Ruth, Tamar), through whom God guarantees the messianic line.

The women prophets understand Yahweh's "partiality." They know that it serves life. For this reason they are not afraid of getting involved and risking danger (Deborah), nor are they preoccupied about protecting their reputations (Tamar). They serve a greater cause and they are faithful to this end. This brings us to the question of persecution. We know that many of the great prophets were persecuted and many were martyred. What happened to the women prophets? This will be the subject of our last point.

Risk of Life Itself: Death-Resurrection

In our study of the women prophets we do not find so much that they were persecuted as that they risked their lives for the life of the people.

At a time when the men were afraid to confront their powerful enemy, Deborah called Barak and then accepted his condition: she accompanied him to the battle with the warning that if she did so, the glory of the victory would belong to a woman (Judg. 4:8–9). Jael, too, risked her life by inviting Sisera to come into her tent (4:18). Judith entered into the enemy's camp and sat defenseless before the awful Holofernes. Her strategy could easily have been discovered (Jth. 10–13). Esther was also aware of the risk of her action: ". . . I shall go to the king in spite of the law; and if I perish, I perish" (Esther 4:16b).

On another level, Ruth accepts every risk when she decides to accompany her mother-in-law with no guarantee of economic security or survival through family descendants. Her decision was final: ". . . where you die, I will die and there will I be buried" (Ruth 1:17a).

In taking the risks she took, the mother of the Maccabees not only exposed herself to danger but also exposed her children. Her courageous stance marks another kind of prophetic martyrdom for women. Often the martyrdom of women means watching their children die for the beliefs they have passed on to them. Isn't this a type of martyrdom? This was the martyrdom of Mary, the mother of Jesus. The mother of the Maccabees watched each of her sons die cruel tortured deaths before she herself was killed (2 Maccabees 7).

Persecution and martyrdom are scarcely mentioned in the accounts of the women prophets. Could it be that we are only given accounts of the women prophets whose work was successful? How many women were martyred anonymously, like the concubine of the levite from Ephraim (Judges 19)?

And what about the heroic work of women today? Don't those women who act as spokespersons for the people have the same qualities as the women prophets of the Hebrew Bible? We believe that they do, and we invite a comparison.

The Prophetic Movement of Women in the Bible as It Is Lived Out in Latin America Today

All over Latin America today we find popular movements searching for creative ways to reclaim their rights. Women play a large role in these movements and often have the responsibility of leaders. We are reminded of Ruth when we see small groups of farmers, including women and children, "invading the land"; that is, squatting on abandoned or fallow tracts, demonstrating their right to have a place to live and fields to plant.

The following testimony of one of the mothers of the Plaza de Mayo symbolizes the people's resistance:

> We show that it is possible to fight in a nonviolent way (and keep in mind that we are not pacifists), against the evil of the

> dictators, gaining small victories every day. The struggle for freedom, justice, and life is over and above ideology, religion, race. In time, truth will overcome.[28]

We could give many more examples. Latin American women leaders and martyrs are as numerous as the violations against the rights of the poor. Usually it is women who cry out. Who can forget the cries of the women of Nicaraugua: "We want peace!" and "Pray for our dead!" These cries still echo in our ears and in our hearts.

To the cries of the oppressed, the base Christian communities respond with songs of hope:

> We are joyful because we know that one day all
> our people will be liberated.
> Our hopes will be realized because Jesus Christ is
> the Savior of the world.

And, these hopes will be realized because faith in the God of Judith is alive and constantly reborn in the midst of the most humble poor.

We need not be afraid that the poor will lose sight of the Gospel; it is continually being rediscovered in their reflections on the texts. On the day of her confirmation, Carmen, a young Peruvian woman from one of the shanty towns of Lima, gave this testimony:

> God is someone who helps us believe we are valuable and who helps us fight for what we need. Freedom is not our goal: anyone who takes up the struggle is already free. Whenever we run up against criticism, slander, and failure we go back to the Word of God where we are told: "I am always with you."

Conclusion

The women prophets of the Hebrew Bible are of the same prophetic line as Jesus.[29] Theirs is a prophetic ministry dedicated to life and the reconstruction of life—in spite of threats and danger. The women who came out of Israel embodied the desire to live, the people's energy, their past, the reasons for their hope: in short, their faith in the covenant with their God. Like Jesus' prophetic ministry, the ministry of these women was a ministry of life. Where there was death and sterility, they demonstrated the strength and value of living. We believe that this same attitude is reborn today in a surprising way in the struggle of the Latin American people and their many women leaders. It is a tireless struggle; it is rooted in faith.

8

I Sense God in Another Way

Consuelo del Prado

The characteristic contribution of the feminine experience of spirituality is born and developed among poor Christians. It is here that it is fed, given light, warmth, and companionship. It is from here that it questions what remains of the shadows, cold, and alienation of our old way of living the faith.

When we speak of the feminine perspective we are referring to an accent, not proposing a polarization. Nevertheless, that accent must be strong enough to emphasize the just claim of the silent or neglected aspects of ordinary speech. In this respect, the comment made by Matilde, the wife of Fermín, who was one of the protagonists in José María Arguedas' novel, *Todas las Sangres* (All Blood), seems appropriate: "I sense God in another way." This phrase demands the right to sense, and thus also to express our distinct experience of God differently.

Spirituality is a way of living; it is also a way of following Jesus. According to Luke, in addition to the twelve disciples who followed Jesus, there were a number of women who followed him. If I were to speculate on the traits of women's way of following Je-

---

Translated from Spanish by Jeltke Aukema.

sus, I would propose two general but fundamental distinctions: women tend to live things out in a more unified way, and they value daily life without giving undue emphasis to isolated moments. These two characteristics indicate a "natural predisposition" to understanding spirituality globally without leaving out any of life's dimensions or facets. The younger generation believes that this emphasis is very important.

Using our particular accents means we will be available to contribute to the entire community. And this community will grow stronger as a community of disciples in the dialogue of giving and feeling. Perhaps now it is clearer why I stated earlier that the objective is not to polarize but emphasize certain aspects.

The three parts of this presentation attempt to propose some other characteristics of feminine spirituality:

- *Suffering*. This defines the circumstances of Latin American women in the poorest sectors.
- *Strength*. This essentially defines them as women of courage.
- *Thankfulness*. The ability to give thanks which is expressed in and strengthens the rich spirituality it inspires.

I Am a Woman Who Suffers

The women in the poorest sectors of Latin America, their souls full of grief and resentment, like Hannah in the temple in Shiloh (cf. 1 Samuel 1:10–13), cry to the Lord. They are women who suffer.

Doubly Exploited

The Puebla document speaks about the indigenous, peasant, working, and marginalized women of the cities as being "doubly exploited and marginalized" (n. 1135, notes). Our work in these areas confirms the truth of this statement.

Women of the poorer sectors suffer and weep much over their situation. They live in an estranged world. They are torn from their land; they are deprived of their schools, their language, and their traditional clothing as well as their children, spouses, and their place in the community. If poverty is death then poor women confront many deaths in their lifetime: the death from hunger, sickness, repression, the death of their traditions, and of their deepest femininity.

The Call for Life

One day while I was attending a neighborhood celebration of the Señor de los Milagros (the Lord of Miracles) in Lima, I heard the beautiful prayer of a woman asking the Lord for health and life for her family members, for the orphans and widows of the country, and especially for those who lived in the area of Ayachucho where there is so much pain and death. This woman, in spite of her own suffering, was aware of the pain of others. She felt called to give up her individualism for the community.

There are many women in the poor sectors who, like this woman, go from their own experience of poverty and need to serve the community, often through their commitment to organizations set up to help others. Living this way gives them a new sense of the God of Life because it demands that they give up their individualism for the good of the community where they feel they are worth something and their lives and experiences are appreciated. This is what is meant by the living God's call to life in abundance.

Comfort My People

The knowledge that she is doubly exploited does not drive the poor woman to self-pity, apathy, or desperation. It is true that such knowledge could be used as an excuse to escape into religion and feel sorry for oneself. Yet, in opening up to the pain of other poor people there is a communion in others' suffering which allows transcendence of one's own pain. So it is that hope and joy is spread among the poorest.

In his writings, José María Arguedas is acutely aware of women's different psychological tones; he provides a magnificent description of a poor crippled Indian woman:

> . . . Gertrude sings like an angel. Though not knowing God, she is known by him. Who else could have given her this voice that washes sin away. It comforts the sad and makes

the happy think. It cleanses the blood of any impurity. God of all, it is not fair to make suffering without consolation. *(María Elena's Testimony)*

In our town there are many Gertrudes who bear their suffering; they are renewed with the consolation that comes to them from a spirituality lived with liberating force. They comfort their people and thus contribute to their own liberation, just as Isaiah did (cf. Isa. 40:1).

The joy that conquers suffering, that does not buckle under pain, persecution, hunger, death, and martyrdom, lives on in a resurrection spirituality that comforts the sad and makes the happy reflect.

The Strong Woman: Who Will Find Her?

A Man's Ideal?

The book of Proverbs paints a picture of a man's ideal woman, "the perfect housewife." Beyond what we find in the description, which must be a man's projection of women, we are interested in the word "strong." This refers to a strength that is not masculine—contrary to what one might think when the text tells us "such a woman has a manly spirit."

In solidarity and service, Latin American women are forging a courage that will allow them to keep going, in spite of poverty and suffering, in their struggle for life and love.

Religious pictures of the crucifixion portray a self-possessed Mary bearing the cup of suffering as she stands at the foot of the cross. This strong woman is an example of so many others who, weighed down by children and pain, also bear the cross of the poor, and helps them on their way. In this shared Calvary, women stay strong and inspire strength in their fellow travelers.

In Love There Is No Fear

Yet until she has arrived at this ideal point in human and spiritual experience, a woman must overcome not just one but many fears. She must break with the old habits ingrained in her to keep silent and withstand anything. She must fight against the little voice inside of her that says: "I'm not worth anything. I can't. I don't know."

When she is called to follow the Lord, she must be converted. This means conversion to solidarity. She must break with a history of personal humiliation in order to open the way for freedom. This is the story of many housewives who, after years of difficulties and oppression, have been converted into free women who work together. Think of the many mothers of those who were "disappeared" in Argentina and other countries of this continent, who undertook a quest from which neither outward repression nor their own inner "weakness" could restrain them.

What allows us to overcome fear is the spirit of love. There is an intense relationship between love, pardon, and freedom. Christ told Peter that whoever forgives much, loves much. And whoever loves much, fears little.

Women in Community

Moving from solitude to community is an act of love; but this is not easily done. Mary, after having consented to God's plans, felt alone because she did not understand God's plans for her Son. The prayer which she offered in her heart allowed her to be open to communion with her Son on the cross. Guarding things in one's heart and opening oneself to communion are two poles which help maintain a healthy tension of feminine strength in the Church, and in one's own spiritual life.

Catherine of Siena, who was known for her constant dialogue with God, was also open to the demands of others; even the appeals of clergy seeking a fuller communion. This is the role of women in the ecclesial community. In the quest for a deeper spirituality with a more personal relationship with Christ, there is always the need for a messenger; Mary Magdalene assumed this role when she brought news of the resurrection to the others. The richness of the message we bring to the community depends much on the profundity of our dialogue with the Lord. This dialogue will be richer if we meditate in solitude on the challenges, questions, and gifts we receive from the community.

Opening ourselves up to communion is a great calling, our highest aspiration; at the same time it is a challenge. Only in realizing this aspiration will we find out how valuable communion is. In the Book of Ruth, the women of Bethlehem tell Naomi that the communion offered by Ruth is more valuable to her than seven sons. Only in community can we overcome the fear that clings to our life. Only in communion will we be able to live out the solidarity to which the poor and Christ call us. Like Mary, we will respond most fully to the Word of God when we step out of ourselves and into the plenitude of communion.

My Soul Proclaims the Greatness of the Lord

The kind of spirituality exemplified by Mary's prayer is essential for a solid Christian life. Saint Teresa of Jesus describes prayer as a covenant of friendship with someone whom we know loves us. If we take human love as a reference, we have a better understanding of the place prayer should have in our lives.

The Explosion of the Word

Mary's Magnificat is the prayer of a poor woman, a believer, and a mother; it is a paradigm for our prayers. All the feminine dimensions of Mary's life are caught up and presented in this song of gratitude and humility, of solidarity and hope, of love and faith. After the angel's visit, Mary spent some time in silence; it was a time of growth, meditation, and commitment. Her visit to Elizabeth was a time of fullness. The atmosphere of solidarity and service provided the proper context for her explosion of gratitude and praise. Silence is always full when it is actively present with others and God. The words prepared in a time like this may explode in joyful celebration at some other time. The Christmas liturgy reminds us that when a profound silence reigns over the earth we can hear the Word of God as a call to fullness. We are privileged with an extraordinary closeness to God because the Word became flesh.

Often, it is in the atmosphere of liturgical celebrations in the poor communities that the silence of women is broken by the most beautiful prayers. We have frequently heard "masterpieces" of prayer, like Mary's which are written into the history of the salvation of the poor. In these prayers thanks is given for the gifts the woman has received from the Lord, and a confession is made of her faith and hope in the God who liberates.

Praise Be to You, O Lord, for Making Me a Woman

Paul Evdokimov says that in an ancient Jewish prayer men pray: ''Praise be to you, O Lord *(Adonai),* for not making me a woman.'' This same feeling is reflected in the writing of Teresa of Jesus who, in describing her spirituality and prayer life, again and again asks for forgiveness on account of her feminine condition. There are many sequels to this way of feeling and praying. Spirituality then, must fight against women's self-concepts as well as a machismo which enslaves and paralyzes women's gifts and creativity.

Giving thanks to God for having made us women means accepting our identity completely. It also presumes that we are willing to recognize the capabilities we must develop. It means that we see ourselves as full of grace—grace upon grace, grace freely given by God—and that we receive all these gifts with humility.

There is one among these gifts that our people really need. We are consecrated in God's tenderness. Without usurping this revelation for ourselves, we know that we are the recipients of God's treasures. It is hard for a woman to forget her child; but sometimes this happens. The Lord does not forget about us. Yet, among the poor, when a woman forgets about her child, and many other women appear who are willing to take in ''just one more,'' one more lost, lonely, sick child to worry over and with whom to share the bread warmed by their love, it is the Lord's doing. Feminine tenderness is a constant reminder of the Father's care. John Paul I expressed this in another way when he said that God is Father and also Mother.

In our context, this presents us with a new way of living love, that is, in productive service. It is not necessary that this productivity be ''imprisoned'' within the bounds of politics. We are in a position to encourage the efficacy of the gratuitous and harvest the fruit of love where no love was sown. Like Judith, we are sure that God is first in our plans and projects, and we can proclaim that there are no conditions on God's plans; in love and power, God can revise them at will.

We find that symbols too are useful for deeper understanding of reality, people, and God. Far beyond the world that is expressed in rational and abstract categories is a universe of profound meaning that is revealed only through beautiful symbolic language. In this universe, we never completely understand the meaning of things; they always appear new and provocative.

Symbolic language is most appropriate for communicating important things that are not visible to the naked eye. It is also wise to use symbolic language in our prayers and liturgical celebrations because it beautifully expresses for God and the community the rich multiformity of creation.

Spiritual Infancy

We welcome with humility this rich experience of gratuity *(gratuidad)* that we receive from the Lord. Only with such an experience can we, like Thérèse of Lisieux, sing the love of the Lord in our lives. Spiritual infancy means that we are dependent upon the Lord, like a baby in its mother's arms. The heart with lofty ambitions and the eyes that look too high, concerns about great affairs and marvels beyond my scope—these do not belong to a spirituality centered in love.

We must learn this lesson every day. Teresa of Jesus often refers to the importance of such experience in the spiritual journey:

> . . . above all, it is necessary to perfect experience because the soul will often be tempted to compromise with whoever deals with it. . . . I think that there are few who are above the experience of such things; thus, it is up to the rest to correct without worrying or hurting . . .[1]

Among the humble and simple women of our people we find masters of this spirituality; what is revealed to them remains hidden from the wise and learned.

Conclusions

A Life Style

The spirituality that concerns us and to which we want to contribute is simply the kind of life of the women who walk "hobbled'' with the poor (to use José María Arguedas' phrase) in following Jesus.

This road is a road of freedom; so it is that the quality of our spirituality may increase with the depth of our experience of freedom. Nevertheless, this freedom becomes real only in surrender and service to our brothers and sisters. Faith, hope, and love are the components of a freedom that is not merely individual, but that denotes the fullness of love. Thus, it is a freedom that we receive as a gift to a child: Only if it is from God will we be truly free and responsible. The particular traits of this kind of life are produced in the process of living it. We see more and more women converted to greater solidarity with the poor. These are women who are joyful in spite of the suffering which cannot dry their fountain of joy. These are humble women who are open to community from their own experience of solitude, and who enrich it with the gifts they have been given freely and who learn to give freely what they have received. These are women who are responsible in their roles in history and have discovered the value and the efficacy of the unconditional. Women who are warm, welcoming, and creative in the way they come to the Lord and to their brothers and sisters.

Mary's Style

When Mary is called the first disciple, she is not resting on her laurels as the mother of Christ, nor on the special role in the history of salvation which she was given by God. We discover her role in the Church and in our own spirituality.

Mary brings us to the Lord for in her we find the perfect model of faithfulness to the Word. She is the disciple who listens and puts the will of the Lord into practice. And in this is rooted the blessedness of her motherhood as Jesus pointed out (Luke 8:21).

A woman of the people, a believer and mother, Mary becomes for us a companion on the road in following her Son. So it is that we are taught the piety of Mary which is so deeply rooted in our continent. We can reclaim her name for our spirituality; in the best sense of the word, our spirituality is Marian.

The Feminine Contribution

Christian spirituality is deeply enriched when we develop the gifts received from the Lord. We have received and been enriched by a wealth of spirituality which is born in our poor believing community and is nourished by the testimony of disciples such as those born each day on this continent through the experience of following Christ.

We have something of ourselves to give to the Christian community and we must do it in the appropriate idiom. Our contribution, marked by our accents, will be received into the church that calls us its disciples. We would do well to make use of our own spirituality and theology, that which flows from those whom we have called the "masters of spirituality," much in the same way the book of Proverbs advises: "Drink the water from your own cistern, fresh water from your own well."

9

Theology from the Perspective of Women

Final Statement: Latin American Conference Buenos Aires, Argentina, Oct. 30–Nov. 3, 1985

God's happiness is like a woman, who, having lost a drachma, lights her lamp and goes about sweeping the whole house, carefully searching until she finds it, and then calls all her friends and neighbors to share her joy at having found it (see Luke 15:8–10).

The drachma symbolizes our self-encounter and self-discovery through our experience of God and through our theological work that we experience in our daily lives. This experience continues to expand until it becomes a celebration in the public square in which every woman is invited to dance and to express herself joyfully in a language all can understand.

Buenos Aires, the capital of Argentina, has been the site of this celebration in which we have shared different ways of searching for

---

Translated from Spanish by Phillip Berryman.

our drachma, our different ways of doing theology. Twenty-eight of us women, from different churches and from nine countries of Latin America and the Caribbean, sought to share, from the woman's viewpoint, different aspects of the riches present in theology, reflecting the different ways this activity is carried out.

There has been enormous diversity of experiences, colors, and shadings. Within this diversity we have found common characteristics, some of which we had not foreseen.

We see that women's theological activity strives to be:

—Unifying, bringing together different human dimensions: strength and tenderness, happiness and tears, intuition and reason.

—Communitarian and relational, bringing together a vast number of experiences that express something lived and felt, in such a way that people recognize themselves in this reflection and feel challenged by it.

—Contextual and concrete, its starting point being the geographical, social, cultural, and ecclesial reality of Latin America, which detects the community's vital issues. This theological activity bears the mark of the everydayness of life as a site where God is made manifest.

—Militant, in the sense of taking part in the totality of our peoples' struggles for liberation at local and global levels.

—Marked by a sense of humor, joy, and celebration, virtues that safeguard the certainty of faith in the God who is with us.

—Filled with a spirituality of hope whose starting point is our situation as women, and which expresses strength, suffering, and thanksgiving.

—Free, with the freedom of those who have nothing to lose; and open, capable of accepting different challenges and contributions.

—Oriented toward refashioning women's history, both in the biblical texts and in those figures of women, who, acting out of their own situation, are symbols of struggle and resistance, wisdom and leadership, solidarity and fidelity, justice and peace.

We have discovered these characteristics, fully aware that it is the Holy Spirit who arouses us and moves us. The same Spirit draws us women out of our own lack of self-esteem and out of the oppression we experience because of our gender, toward an effort to break out of old frameworks, and to build a new person (woman/

man) and a new society. All of this we experience out of our commitment to the poor, struggling for our common liberation.

In our celebration in Buenos Aires, we inquired into what methods and what mediations we utilized in our theological activity. We were surprised to note that the characteristics that we discovered amount to our own method, and the mediations embrace a whole range of possibilities that can take expression in many languages. Social sciences, psychology, linguistics, philosophy, sociology of religion, ecology, and other sciences are present there and are woven together with the Bible, Tradition, and Life in a single tapestry, vibrant with color and hope. What is expressed is our unifying and inclusive way of perceiving life.

We work in a constant process of breaking away, as though in an ongoing childbirth, in which we seek to release ourselves from old frameworks and from categories imposed by the patriarchal system, in order to give birth to something closer to life, something more densely packed with meaning for us.

We have discovered that we can widen the horizon of our theological reflection in different directions, taking on different religious expressions, and taking into account the problem of racial discrimination as well as social justice.

We have realized that certain themes must be deepened from the woman's viewpoint, themes such as the image of God, the incarnation, the experience of God, the Trinity, community, the body, suffering and joy, conflict and silence, the ludic and the political, tenderness and beauty.

As a sign of this work as a group, we have accepted responsibility for certain tasks:

—To seek a synthesis in our ongoing formation between cultural values—those practices aimed at changing the situation—and "theories" that operate on different levels of human life.

—To pay attention to the theological experience and reflection that is taking place in base-level groups, especially by women, to take on this experience and to allow ourselves to be challenged by it in the process of a mutual enrichment, while also making our contribution.

—To systematize and transmit our experience and reflection.

—To seek, from this theological perspective, common paths with men, helping them to see the strength and tenderness that are part of the common task of bringing forth and nourishing the life of the new person—woman/man—and the new society.

When we conclude this conference, we shall be taking many questions away with us, to nourish our lives and to help enlighten our search.

The joy of the woman who found her drachma was full only when she was able to share it. In this sense, we want to share our discoveries and hopes with all our colleagues, women and men, and particularly with the women and men theologians of the Ecumenical Association of Third World Theologians (EATWOT) who sponsored our conference.

Notes

Introduction: *The Power of the Naked*

1. This account of the story is taken from *Tenochtitlán en una isla* by Ignacio Bernal (Mexico: Fondo de Cultura Económica, SEP, 1984), pp. 84–86.

2. The phrase "God-talk" is used by Gustavo Gutiérrez in his book *On Job* (Maryknoll, N.Y.: Orbis Books, 1987).

3. I. Bernal, p. 90.

4. Ibid., p. 91.

1. *Women and the Theology of Liberation*

1. Michel de Certeau, *La escritura de la historia* (Mexico City: Universidad Iberoamericana, 1985).

2. M. Zapata, "El hombre colombiano," in *Enciclopedia del Desarrollo Colombiano,* vol. 1 (Bogotá, 1974).

3. Otto Maduro, "Extraction de la plus-valia: Répression de la sexualité et Catholicisme in Amérique Latine," *Liaisons Internationales,* 32 (1982): 18ff.

4. Jean-Marie Aubert, *La femme* (Paris, 1975), pp. 109ff.

5. Workers' leader and Brazilian Jocist director Angelina de Oliveira told us that up until 1956 the activists of the Brazilian JOC could not be engaged to be married, as this would mean not having enough time for the movement. See Ana María Bidegain de Uran, "Sexualidad, vida religiosa y situación de la mujer in América Latina," *Texto y Contexto* (Bogotá: Universidad de los Andes), no. 7 (January–April 1986).

6. Magdala Velásquez, "Aspectos históricos de la condición de la mujer en Colombia," *Voces Insurgentes* (Bogotá, 1976).

7. Ana María Bidegain, "La organización de movimientos de Juventud de Acción Católica en América Latina," thesis presented for the doctorate in historical sciences (Louvain; Université Catholique de Louvain, 1979).

8. Gustavo Gutiérrez, *A Theology of Liberation,* rev. ed. (Maryknoll, N.Y.: Orbis Books, 1988), p. ix; first italics added. Originally *Teología de la liberación: Perspectivas* (Lima: CEP, 1971).

9. Leonardo Boff, *The Maternal Face of God* (San Francisco: Harper & Row, 1987).

10. The group of laity called together by the Pontifical Council for the Laity to help prepare for the last synod (held at Rocca di Papa, May 1987), posed many of the themes that I am about to take up here. Although I was not elected by the bases of the movements or national churches (as we know, the organization of the Church is not democratic), nevertheless the various tendencies and experiences of the Latin American Church were represented, by and large, and their reflections seem to me to be representative of that very broad ecclesial spectrum.

11. Rosa D. Trapaso, *The Feminization of Poverty* (Latin America Press, 1984); Thomas J. Kniesner, B. J. McElroy, and Steven Wilcox, "Family Structure, Race, and Feminization of Poverty," *Working Papers in Economics* (Duke University); see especially *Concilium* (Spanish edition), 1987, no. 214, *Las mujeres, el trabajo y la pobreza.*

4. *Reflections on the Trinity*

1. For example: Leonardo Boff, *The Maternal Face of God* (San Francisco: Harper & Row, 1987); R. Haughton, "Is God Masculine?" *Concilium* 134 (1980): 63–70; C. Halkes, "The Themes of Protest in Feminine Theology against God the Father," *Concilium* 134 (1980): 103–112; Rosemary Radford Ruether, "The Feminine Nature of God," *Concilium* 143 (1981): 61–68; M. Hunt, R. Gibellini, *La sfida del femminismo alla teologia* (Brecia: Ed. Queriniana, 1980).

2. K. E. Borresen, "L'anthropologie théologique d'Augustin et de Thomas d'Aquin," *Recherches de Science Religieuse* 69/3 (1981): 394.

3. Ibid., p. 397.

4. We won't deal here with the other ecclesiastical, that is, sacramental, aspects which are directly related to this issue such as the fact that women are not allowed to perform priestly functions simply because they are female. We believe that these themes, in spite of their importance, go beyond the bounds of this article.

5. L. Boff, p. 84.

6. E. and J. Moltmann, *Dieu, homme et femme* (Paris: Ed. du Cerf, 1984), p. 132.

7. C. Halkes, p. 123.

8. V. Jenni-Westermann, *Theologisches Handwörterbuch zum Alten Testament,* II, pp. 761–68.

9. *Dives in Misericordia,* III, note 52.

10. See also Pss. 25:6; 40:12; 51:3; 69:17; 79:8; 103:4; 106:46; 119:77; 145:9; 156; Lam. 3:22; Dan. 9:9, 18; and others.

11. See also Jenni-Westermann, p. 768.

12. G. Philips, "Le Saint Esprit et Marie—Le Vatican II cet prospective du problème," *Bulletin de la Soc. Fr. d'Etudes Mariales,* 1 (1968): 30.

13. P. Evdokimov, "La maternité théandrique—figure de la paternité divine," "Panagion et Panagia," *Bulletin de la Soc. Fr. d'Etudes Mariales,* 3 (1970): 65.

14. Cf. G. Philips, p. 30.

15. R. Haughton, p. 64.

16. R. R. Ruether, p. 63.

17. Cf. S. Bulgakov, *The Wisdom of God* (London: Paisley Press, 1937).

18. Cf. G. Kittel, *The Theological Dictionary of the New Testament,* vol. 1 (Grand Rapids: Eerdmans, 1964), p. 141.

19. Ibid.

20. We are aware of the danger of seeking tendentiously a reversal of dominations which could result in an inverted "theological sexology."

21. Cf. note 1 in *The Jerusalem Bible.*

22. L. Boff, p. 81.

23. P. Benoit and M. E. Boismare, *Synopse des quatre évangiles en français,* vol. 1 (Paris, 1981), p. 153.

24. Cited from E. Pagels, "God the Father, God the Mother," *The Gnostic Gospels* (New York: Random House, 1979), pp. 67–68.

25. Cf. M. Lindstrom, *Julian of Norwich and the Motherhood of God* (Minnesota), pp. 204–205.

26. Julian of Norwich, *Showings* (New York: Paulist Press, 1978), p. 279.

27. Ibid., p. 292.

28. Ibid., pp. 296–97.

29. Cf. M. Lindstrom, p. 208.

30. L. Boff, p. 65.

31. Cf. R. Laurentin, "Jesus e as mulheres—una revolucão ignorada," *Concilium* 154 (1980): 84.

32. Cf. L. Boff, p. 92.

33. E. and J. Moltmann, p. 58.

34. Cf. experience of Julian of Norwich.

35. Here we could also talk about the mystery of Mary; but let us leave this for another work.

36. Cf. L. Boff, op. cit.

37. Cf. what was said above about this biblical word.

38. H. M.-Manteau, O. P. Bonamuy, "L'Esprit Saint, divine Mère du Christ?" "Et la Vierge concut du Saint Esprit," *Bulletin de la Soc. Fr. d'Etudes Mariales*, (1970): 18.

39. Ibid.

40. E. and J. Moltmann, p. 120.

41. Cf. J. Moltmann, "The Motherly Father: Is Trinitarian Patripassianism Replacing Theological Patriarchalism?" *Concilium* 143 (1981): 54, and L. Boff, op. cit.

42. Cf. H. M. Manteau, O. P. Bonamuy, p. 22.

43. Cf. Puebla 291.

44. E. and J. Moltmann, p. 136.

45. Ibid., pp. 105–106.

46. See the rabbinic writings for the theological use of word *Shekinah*. F. Rosensweig, "L'étoile de la rédemption," (Paris: Ed. du Seuil, 1982).

47. J. Moltmann, p. 54.

48. K. E. Borresen, p. 403.

49. Ibid., p. 404.

50. Cf. Saint Gregory Nazianzus.

51. E. and J. Moltmann, p. 118.

52. The term is E. and J. Moltmann's, ibid., p. 122.

5. *Women and Christology*

1. Jon Sobrino, *Jesus in Latin America* (Maryknoll, N.Y.: Orbis Books, 1987), p. 9.

2. Sobrino, p. 3.

3. Much has been written about the role of the different christologies in the conquest and subjugation of the Latin American continent as well as about how the "internalization" of certain christological images facilitated domination. For further reading on this subject we suggest "Christología Conquista-Colonizatíon" by Saul Trinidad in *Jésus: Ni Vencido, Ni Monarca Celestial*, ed. J. M. Bonino (Buenos Aires: Ed. Terra Nueva, 1977).

4. Sobrino, p. 59.

5. Hebe Bonafini, from a report that appeared in *La Voz Semanal*, Sunday supplement, June 16, 1985.

6. J. Sobrino, p. 54.

7. Leonardo Boff, *The Maternal Face of God* (San Francisco: Harper & Row, 1987), p. 132.

8. Gustavo Gutiérrez, *A Theology of Liberation* (Maryknoll, N.Y.: Orbis Books, 1973), p. 198.

9. G. Gutiérrez, p. 202.

10. L. Boff, op. cit.

11. These testimonies are registered in a publication of the Permanent Assembly for Human Rights which condemned the presentations of several women participating in a roundtable discussion on "Women and Human Rights," Buenos Aires, March 16, 1984.

12. Giorgio Girardet, *A los Cautivos Libertad* (Buenos Aires: Ed. Tierra Nueva), p. 106.

13. Author's paraphrase.

6. Women and the People of God

1. Johannes Bauer, *Encyclopedia of Biblical Theology* (New York: Sheed and Ward, 1961), p. 103.

2. Joachim Jeremias, *New Testament Theology* (New York: Scribner's, 1971), p. 168.

3. Ibid., p. 170.

4. Gustavo Gutiérrez, *A Theology of Liberation*, rev. ed. (Maryknoll, N.Y.: Orbis Books, 1988), p. 90.

5. J. Jeremias, p. 178.

6. Juan Luis Segundo, *The Community Called Church* (Maryknoll, N.Y.: Orbis Books, 1973), p. 4f.

7. J. Bauer, p. 107.

8. J. L. Segundo, p. 13.

9. Gustavo Gutiérrez, *The Power of the Poor in History* (Maryknoll, N.Y.: SCM Press/Orbis Books, 1983), p. 25.

10. Julio Barreiro, *Nuevas dimensiones para la misión de la Iglesia en América Latina* (Buenos Aires: Ed. Tierra Nueva, 1977), p. 6.

11. Horacio Schultais, "Articulo del Estandarte Evangélico," *El problema de la dueda externa.*

12. José Comblin, "El tema de la liberatión en el pensamiento latinoamericano," an article published by the SELADOC Team (Salamanca: Sígueme, 1975), p. 242.

7. The Prophetic Ministry of Women in the Hebrew Bible

1. Cf. VV. AA., "Inciniacao à análise estrutural," *Cuadernos Bíblicos*, no. 23 (São Paulo: Ed. Paulinas, 1983).

2. Clodovis Boff, *Teología e Prática* (Petrópolis: Vozes, 1978), pp. 249–50. English translation: *Theology and Praxis* (Maryknoll, N.Y.: Orbis Books, 1987).

3. Carlos Mesters, *Flor sem defensa* (Petrópolis: Vozes, 1983), p. 59.

English translation: *Defenseless Flowers* (Maryknoll, N.Y.: Orbis Books, 1989).

4. An example of this is seen in the exclamation of a poor woman who said "You don't need to leave Ceará to understand the Bible!"

5. For example, in 2 Sam. 14:1ff., a "quick-witted" woman from Tekoa is called by Joab to go to David and intercede for Absalom. Later (2 Sam. 20:14ff.), a wise woman intervenes in the battle between a town and Joab. She saves the town by convincing him to do what is right. Queen Esther (chapter 4) comes on the scene at a time when the people of Israel are threatened with extinction. In this dramatic account, she makes a decision and so opts for life and solidarity with her people.

6. John F. Craghan, "Esther, Judith, and Ruth: Paradigms of Human Liberation," *Journal of Bible and Theology, Biblical Theology Bulletin,* vol. 12, no. 1 (January 1982): 12.

7. Ibid., p. 18.

8. Already in Egypt we find midwives defying Pharaoh's order by protecting the lives of Israel's baby boys.

9. Rosa Marga Rothe, "Duas mulheres violentas: Débora e Jael," *A violência dos oppressores e o direito dos pobres à vida na Bíblia,* Estudos Biblicos, no. 6 (Petrópolis: Vozes), pp. 21–30.

10. Carlos Mesters, *Rute, uma histórica da Bíblia* (Sao Paulo: Ed. Paulinas, 1985).

11. For more on the process of capitulation and death on the one hand and reaction and life on the other, see Craghan, p. 11. The narrative in Judith, along with those found in Ruth and Esther, form a movement of disorientation, so that the people might be *reoriented* toward life. This is what happens in liberation.

12. Sandro Gallazzi, "Os Macabeus: uma luta pela liberdade do povo," *A violência dos opressores e o direito dos pobres à vida, na Bíblia,* Estudos Bíblicos, no. 6 (Petrópolis: Vozes, 1985), p. 47.

13. The Hebrew root *re'a* (Ruth) denotes the personification of love in solidarity with one's neighbor.

14. Milton Schwantes, "Profecia e organizção: Anotacoes à luz de um texto (Amos 2:6–16)," *Bíblia e organização popular,* Estudos Bíblicos, no. 6 (Petrópolis: Vozes, 1985), p. 33.

15. This citation is from 2 Timothy. 1:5 where Paul reminds Timothy of the faith of his mother and grandmother: a faith without doubt that lives in the heart.

16. These ideas are repeated throughout Carlos Mesters' work. Gustavo Gutiérrez affirms: ". . . it is precisely this faith and hope in the God of the people that makes us the people of God." *La fuerza histórica de los*

pobres (Lima: CEP, 1979). English translation: *The Power of the Poor in History* (Maryknoll, N.Y.: Orbis Books, 1983).

17. Hugo Echegaray, "Derecho del pobre, derecho de Dios," *Dios de los sencillos,* Colección Páginas, no. 3 (Lima: CEP, 1978), p. 134.

18. Mesters, *Rute,* p. 65.

19. Craghan, p. 1.

20. This cry is found in Yahwist (Exod. 3:7–10), as well as in Priestly tradition (Exod. 2:23–24).

21. Craghan, pp. 12–13. We refer here to the Hebrew edition of the book.

22. In Ruth, knowing the symbolism conveyed by the names is essential to understanding the text. The name *Mara* means "bitter"; *Naomi* means "lucky winner."

23. Mesters, op. cit., p. 35.

24. Elsa Tamez, "A mulher que complicou a história da salvacao," *Por trós da palavra,* Boletím do CEDI, no. 27, March–April 1985.

25. José Comblin, *O Clamor dos oprimidos, o clamor de Jesús* (Petrópolis: Vozes, 1984). English translation: *Cry of the Oppressed, Cry of Jesus* (Maryknoll, New York: Orbis Books, 1988).

26. Cf. footnote in Jerusalem Bible.

27. In regard to the "women of the palace," see Rosa Marga Rothe's comments in her article on Deborah and Jael, pp. 24–27.

28. Hebe Bonafini, president of the "Mothers of the Plaza de Mayo," cf. *Cadernos do 3o Mundo,* no. 80 (June 1985): 48.

29. José Comblin, "Jesús Profeta," Estudos Bíblicos, no. 4 (Petrópolis: Vozes), pp. 41–59.

8. *I Sense God in Another Way*

1. *The Book of Life* (New York and London: Penguin Books, 1957), 40, 8.

Contributors

ANA MARÍA BIDEGAIN was born in Uruguay and is a citizen of Colombia. She is a lay Catholic historian of the Church with a doctorate in history from the Catholic University of Louvain, and currently teaches at the University of the Andes (Bogotá) and Duke University (Durham, N.C.). She is the author of three books: *Nacionalismo, Militarismo y Dominación en America Latina; Iglesia, Pueblo y Politica;* and *Así actuaron los cristianos en la historia de América Latina.*

MARÍA CLARA BINGEMER, a Brazilian lay Catholic theologian, is a professor of theology at the Pontifical Catholic University of Rio de Janeiro and the Santa Ursula University. She is regional coordinator of the Ecumenical Association of Third World Theologians (EATWOT) for Latin America, and is co-author, with J.B. Libanio, of *Christian Eschatology,* and, with Yvonne Gebara, of *Mary: Mother of God, Mother of the Poor,* which will be published by Orbis in 1989.

TEREZA CAVALCANTI teaches biblical pastoral studies at the Catholic University of Rio de Janeiro. She is the author of *A Logica do Amor* on the theology of Carlos Mesters and the coordinator of the Woman and Theology program at the ISER.

IVONE GEBARA, a Roman Catholic Sister from Brazil, is professor of philosophy and theology at the Theological Institute of Recife. Her book co-authored with María Clara Bingemer, *Mary: Mother of God, Mother of the Poor,* will appear in Orbis' Theology and Liberation Series in 1989.

CONSUELO DEL PRADO is a Catholic Sister from Peru.

NELLY RITCHIE, an ordained minister with a licentiate in theology, is superintendent of the Evangelical Methodist Church in Argentina.

ARACELY DE ROCCHIETTI is a Methodist pastor in Uruguay.

ELSA TAMEZ, a Methodist from Mexico, is at present a doctoral candidate at the University of Lausanne, Switzerland. She is author of *The Bible of the Oppressed.*

ALIDA VERHOEVEN, a native of Holland, was ordained in the Argentine Methodist Church, the first woman to be accepted in the pastoral ministry of that denomination. She lives in Mendoza and works with a group of women victims of human rights violations, and their children, at the Ecumenical Foundation of Cuyo, which she helped to organize.

Index

Index